POLAND'S INDE

Solidarity

Poland's
Independent Trade Union

Denis MacShane

Spokesman

First published in 1981 by Spokesman
Bertrand Russell House, Gamble Street, Nottingham NG7 4ET

British Library Cataloguing in Publication Data

MacShane, Denis
Solidarity.
1. Trade-unions — Poland — History
2. Solidarity
I. Title
331.8809438 HD6735.7

ISBN 0 85124 319 3
ISBN 0 85124 318 5 Pbk

Printed by the Russell Press Ltd., Nottingham

To the memory of Jan Matyjaszek, 1916-1958

Contents

Introduction

NSZZ Solidarnosc — in English, the Independent Self-Governing Trade Union Solidarity, came into formal legal existence on 10th November 1980 when its statutes were registered by a Warsaw Court. The new union, formed by Polish workers, has since commanded the world's headlines, but there have been very few accounts of its day-to-day work and its achievements in the workplace. To read many reports of Solidarity is to be given the impression that the union sprang into existence from nowhere in the summer of 1980. In fact, Polish workers have a long tradition of fighting for their rights — rights as producers, as consumers and as Polish citizens. The roots of Solidarity stretch back many years and the working people of Poland have a post-war history of struggle of which they can be proud. I have tried in this short book to explain how Solidarity works and where it has come from.

Since August 1980 each week has brought tremendous changes in Poland which render writing a book about such a rapidly evolving situation a precarious business. But I think it is important that trade unionists and the general public outside of Poland should have the opportunity to read an account which explains the trade union work of Solidarity. Any shop steward or union official from Western Europe or North America parachuted into a Polish workplace would find him- or herself engaged in activity similar to that carried out in trade unions outside of Poland. Poles are both Catholic and nationalist, but Solidarity is an organisation of workers with working-class ambitions. Any Western trade unionist knows that the mass media are unlikely to give trade unions and workers a fair deal in terms of daily coverage. With some exceptions the coverage of Poland has concentrated on the religious, the national, or the political aspects of Solidarity and has ignored its trade union role. As a consequence there are many trade union activists in the West and many socialists who regard Solidarity with suspicion or who have reservations about whether it can be considered a genuine trade union worthy of the fullest support by workers outside Poland. I have never been convinced that there is a clear-cut division between trade union demands and political demands. Solidarity can no more opt out of the political development of Poland than British trade unions can avoid being involved in the Labour Party. Nevertheless, the work of Solidarity is mainly devoted to defending and extending the well-being of its members, their families and the community in which they live. Out of a population of 36 million in Poland, something like 10 million belong to Solidarity. If you add to that figure each worker's dependents, you arrive at about 80 per cent of Poland's population. Consequently Solidarity is obliged to involve itself in a wide range of social and political questions that go beyond the narrowest bread-and-butter economism. To raise points about food distribution, price levels, allocation of funds to build new hospitals, or to criticise managerial inefficiency or corruption and demand that security police buildings are converted for use as kindergartens would seem reasonable trade union preoccupations in the West. In Eastern Europe they challenge the nature of political power and in particular, the control exercised by one party — the Communist Party — over all aspects of economic and social organisation within the State.

I have not tried in this book to describe the political changes that have taken place inside Poland since August 1980. The evolution of the Polish United Workers' Party (Poland's ruling Communist Party) is for someone else to analyse. Overhanging the whole period has been the question of an intervention by the Soviet Union. Between writing these words and this book being published, anything could happen, though most of the Poles I spoke to considered a formal military invasion to be more of a fear in the West than in Poland itself. A Soviet invasion would satisfy those for whom independent, strong, democratically accountable trade unions are an anathema in the West and only acceptable in Poland because they are perceived as a threat to the Soviet Union; for these hypocrites (can there be many more revolting sights than the Thatchers and Reagans of the world praising Polish workers while doing everything in their power to weaken trade unions and increase unemployment in their own countries?) a Soviet invasion would justify a further massive increase in arms spending and would achieve a principal ambition of reactionaries all over the world, that is, the destruction of détente and peaceful East-West dialogue for at least a generation to come.

Another subject to which I have not been able to give full justice is the problem of Poland's agriculture and Poland's peasants. There is another book to be written on Rural Solidarity and how Poland's food production needs can be met. This book concentrates on industrial Solidarity and the industrial working class. As far as possible I have tried to identify my sources by individually quoting the people I have interviewed or citing the document or journal I have taken a quotation from. For anyone interested in

Solidarity the best source material in English is to be found in recent issues of *Labour Focus on Eastern Europe* (available from Box 23, 136 Kingland High Street, London E8) and in the bulletin published by the Information Centre for Polish Affairs (115 Redston Road, London N8) which translates many of Solidarity's statements. In French there is the journal *L'Alternative* (1 place Paul-Painlevé, 75005 Paris) which has carried some excellent interviews with Polish workers and Solidarity leaders and translations of original Solidarity texts and documents. Daniel Singer's marvellous book, *The Road to Gdansk (Monthly Review Press)* is essential reading for the events leading up to August 1980 and the best account I have come across of the Gdansk strike and negotiation.

Most of my information about Solidarity comes from Polish workers themselves and it is to all the people who gave up time to answer my questions that I owe an unrepayable debt of thanks. Elizabeth Jasinska, Helena Luczywo and Liliana Klaptocz helped me cope with one of Europe's loveliest but most impenetrable languages. Mark Cousins, Bronislaw Geremek, Collin Gonze, Tadeusz Kowalik, Jacek Kurczewski, Gienek Smolar and Werner Thönessen either read various sections of this book in draft form or have discussed various problems connected with Poland with me and their comments have been both essential and invaluable. Special thanks to Joyce Beck, Margaret Kasofsky and Gertrude Swedish for typing it so quickly and to Amanda and Tony Holden for friendship and hospitality when finishing the work in Washington. Above all I owe thanks to the General Secretary of the International Metalworkers' Federation, Herman Rebhan, for the help and encouragement he has given me both in writing this book and in fostering my interest in Poland and Solidarity. Although I am an official of the International Metalworkers' Federation this book in no way reflects Federation policy. The errors and the personal interpretations that may be contained in it are all my own responsibility. The object of writing it is to widen understanding about the work of Solidarity as a trade union of workers. During my life as an active trade unionist I can think of no other event that has marked such a victory for working people. In every country where workers are struggling to form effective, independent trade unions to represent their interests the example of Poland is eagerly discussed. And it is an example that tells us clearly that it is only the power of the organised working class that can decisively change society for the better. The workers united, will never be defeated.

Warsaw-Washington-London-Geneva.
May-July 1981.

Chapter 1

May Day 1981, Warsaw

The procession slowly came up Krolewska Street to Victory Square. It was thinner, smaller than usual — more like a May Day parade in Britain than the gigantic processions to be seen in television reports of May Day in Eastern Europe. Some veterans, a few elderly party members, communist youth organisations, a handful of flags. Soldiers lined that part of the square where the tomb of the unknown soldier from the 1939-45 war stood. The procession marched around it before setting off again. Suddenly the onlookers tensed. "It can't be true", whispered my interpreter. But it was. Stanislaw Kania, first secretary of the Polish United Workers' Party and General Wojciech Jaruzelski, Poland's Prime Minister, surrounded by other members of the Politburo and Central Committee members, were leading the procession out of Victory Square to its next stop in Warsaw's Theatre Square.

It had never been seen before in Poland, nor in any other East European State: the party leaders walking modestly at the head of a May Day parade instead of cut off on the giant reviewing stands while the faithful went past below. In fact, so lax was the security and so available were the leaders that, as the crowd swirled around Theatre Square, I found myself only two yards behind Kania and Jaruzelski, walking with Politburo members who looked at me as if it were quite normal to have a total stranger strolling in their midst.

At the far end of Theatre Square a row of pale blue mini-buses was waiting to take off the top leadership to lunch. Television cameramen and journalists jostled to get close to Kania and Jaruzelski. "It is incredible", said Chris Bobinski, the *Financial Times* Warsaw correspondent, "all my life the security police have been keeping me away from Kania and now they're saying: 'Go on, ask him a question. Get closer, hear what he's saying.' "

The reduction in scale in 1981 of the official May Day parades throughout Poland symbolised the loosening of control by the country's rulers. Solidarity had told its members to ignore the official May Day parades and treat the day as a family holiday. The union stressed that in future years it wanted to celebrate 1st May as genuine workers' manifestation of international workers' solidarity, but after 35 years of official, compulsory May Day parades a break was needed.

As the long, thin procession went along its much abbreviated Warsaw route, the effect of Solidarity's edict was obvious. In past years the biggest contingents in the Warsaw parade had been several hundred strong sections from the giant Ursus tractor factory or Warsaw's steel plant, Huta Warszawa. Now there were fewer than twenty Party members to be found ready to march behind the flag of those two important industrial enterprises. Both Ursus and Huta Warszawa are Solidarity strongholds.

The procession was bedraggled. People shuffled along and an event that in previous years lasted from early morning to mid-afternoon was over in a couple of hours. One young man tried to unfurl a banner in the middle of the crowd calling for the release of Poland's political prisoners. He was set upon by some old party members who hustled him towards the militia, beating him all the while. Other people shouted: "Don't hit him. It may be provocation." A very nervous looking 19 year old was handed over to a squad of militia, to be released a few hours later. Again, it could only have happened since August 1980.

August 1980, Gdansk

It will take many years before the significance of August 1980 in Poland is properly understood. But given the point from where they started and the strength of Poland's ruling organisations, coupled with Poland's geo-political position, it is difficult to conceive of any other country in which workers have achieved so much so quickly. The creation of independent trade unions, a major wage increase, improvements in family allowances and pensions, a substantial reduction in working time, release of political prisoners, increased access to the media, reinstatement of victimised workers, all of these amount to major gains which any trade union anywhere in the world would be proud to boast of. To watch television or to read much of the world's press since August 1980 is to be endlessly given details about the religious and nationalist aspects of Solidarity's birth and continuing existence. And certainly the importance of both Polish national consciousness and the Roman Catholic Church cannot be underestimated in any treatment of what has happened, is happening and will happen in Poland. But the victory was a workers' victory and the further achievements since August 1980 have been due to the power of the workers. Lech Walesa and the other Solidarity leaders are surrounded by advisers — intellectuals, politicians, Catholics, atheists, cautious right-wingers and determined socialists — but the decisions they take are their own, based on their own experiences and knowledge as working class representatives.

Unless you own capital there is only one way, once raising

demands and trying to negotiate has been shown to be ineffective, that you can put pressure on capital — that is to strike. It is the only real and effective weapon that workers have. It is why throughout the world, from the most advanced liberal democracies through to authoritarian communist States, to the microchip republics of Asia, or down to the dictatorship and racist regimes of Latin America and South Africa the right to strike is continually under threat in a thousand different ways. Workers have never been given anything. They have always had to fight for what they could win. It is well beyond the scope of this book to discuss the theoretical nature of economic relations in East European States, but the formal State ownership of the means of production did not appear to have convinced the Polish worker that he or she no longer had legitimate demands to put to the employer.

From the beginning of July 1980 workers in Poland had been angry over government attempts to increase food prices and strikes had taken place in the textile centre of Lodz, in the industrial centre of Wroclaw, in Lublin near the Russian border and in Warsaw itself. But for the moment, in Gdansk, centre of a workers' revolt in 1970, the authorities must have felt pretty pleased with themselves. In the Lenin shipyards they had just got rid of a crane driver, Anna Walentynowicz, a known trouble-maker, a stirrer-upper, who on and off since 1970 had been raising workers' demands and organising little localised stoppages of sections of workers inside the shipyard in order to put pressure on the management. She had been declared "mentally ill", and had to fight through the courts to prevent her job from being taken away, but always against opposition from the shipyard management and the official union. On August 6th she went home ill. The next day management dismissed her for "deserting her work post". She was offered a job miles away from Gdansk. At the same time they were happy that another notorious Gdansk trouble-maker, Lech Walesa, was out of work, victimised on account of the number of times he had raised workers' cases with the shipyard management and with other managements in Gdansk.

Anna Walentynowicz's dismissal angered the workers inside the Lenin shipyard. Unlike workers in the rest of Poland, they had stayed calm during the food price rise strikes in July and early August; this, despite the existence of The Committee of Free Trade Unions for the Baltic Coast, formed in May 1978 by, amongst others, Anna Walentynowicz and Andrzej Gwiazda, who was later to become Solidarity's Vice President. Strikes do not explode spontaneously. No worker anywhere in the world stops work, begins losing pay, faces victimisation, without a real sense of grievance and without intense discussion and organisation prior to the strike.

In Gdansk everyone remembered the workers shot dead when the security forces put down the 1970 strike. It was an added reason for caution. Nor do workers, especially not hardened shipyard workers, down tools because of outside agitators or inflammatory speeches by rabble rousing rank and file leaders. There was an active group of workers and intellectuals who had been producing *Robotnik* (The Worker) *of the Coast* which circulated in the Baltic towns of Gdansk, Gdynia, Sopot, Elblag and Szczecin. In May 1980, two organisers of a May 3rd rally in Gdansk, Tadeusz Szczudlowski and Dariusz Kobzdej, had been sentenced to three months' imprisonment for staging a rally. Daily prayer services were held for their release and for the establishment of trade union rights. On 18th June 1980 there was an explosion in the Gdansk dockyards. Eight men died and 60 were injured. Workers complained that inadequate safety precautions had caused the blast.

There was a continuing row in Gdansk over sand-stripping of paintwork. It is an old fashioned and dangerous way of cleaning dirty paint from ships in repair yards. In Poland it is officially banned, but the practice continued. As a Catch 22 consequence, the Gdansk workers could not get the necessary protective clothing because in officialdom's eyes the practice of sand-stripping no longer existed.

The victimisation of the popular Anna Walentynowicz gave the workers a chance to launch a strike in Gdansk that would go far beyond the food price demands of the strikes elsewhere in Poland. At a party on Saturday night 9th August, to celebrate the release of Kobzbej and Sczudlowski, which was attended by most of the Gdansk opposition trade unionists, the idea of launching a strike over Anna Walentynowicz's sacking was discussed. Over the weekend, a group of workers associated with the Committee of Free Trade Unions on the Baltic Coast went to Warsaw for talks with Jacek Kuron and other leaders of KOR. (See Chapter 4 for the history of KOR). They came back with their own ideas of presenting a list of demands that would go a lot further than a wage rise to cover increased food costs and the reinstatement of Anna Walentynowicz. They knew what they wanted. Above all it was the right to elect their own leaders and to form their own union. On Monday 11th August, 6000 leaflets setting out these demands were printed.

That demand may have been clothed in words by intellectuals. Later, during the negotiations over the 21 demands presented by the strikers, the significant choice of *independent* rather than *free* as the key adjective describing the new union would be prompted by an intellectual, after reservations raised by the government side who said that the word *free* was part of the Western trade union world's terminology and would upset the Kremlin far more than the description, *independent*. But the call for trade unions that would be organisations by, for and of the workers came from the workers themselves as a result of their own sense of what they needed.

On Thursday 14th August, the 17,000 workers at the Lenin shipyards went on strike. (See Appendix for two interviews describing events on the morning of 14th August). Soon workers in Gdynia and Sopot struck. By the end of the day, 50,000 workers on the Baltic coast were sitting quietly inside their workplaces. The lessons learned from 1970 were not to leave the workplace, not to demonstrate in the street, not to attack party or official union buildings — simply to stay put and stop production.

Their demands were five-fold: the reinstatement of Anna Walentynowicz and Lech Walesa; the erection of a monument to the dead workers of 1970; a wage increase of 2,000 zlotys (£25 or $60) per month (the average wage was 5,500 zlotys), with increases in family allowances and pensions; cancellation of the meat price rise and the right to form an independent union.

Demands are one thing: finding someone to negotiate them is another. Lech Walesa had been active since the trouble started over the victimisation of Anna Walentynowicz, talking to workers, discussing a possible strike with old friends at the shipyard. He had been one of the 1970 strikers elected as a delegate to meet Edward Gierek in January 1971. On 14th August, he climbed over the railings that surround the Lenin Shipyard and addressed the workers. He was the perfect choice to go and present the demands to management. He could look after himself verbally. They would not pull the wool over his eyes. He was a worker, not an intellectual. He was a devout Catholic, a good family man. He had been arrested dozens of times. Best of all, he had nothing to lose. If it all went horribly wrong, he could not be sacked or demoted and another prison sentence held no fears. Dotted all over the world there are trade unionists like Walesa, men and women whose lives have been destroyed because of their commitment to trade unionism. Normally, they are excoriated by the mass media that have made such a hero of Walesa. But, if one strips away all the excessive Western hero-worship of Walesa, you find a very tough, determined, working class representative, afraid of no one (as he says: "Afraid of no one but God"), equipped with a canny sense of how far to go and which issues to push and which to leave alone. He was in the right place, with the right ideas, at the right time. But if Walesa did not exist, someone else would have filled his role. Thankfully for the Gdasnk Lenin Shipyard workers he was there. Together with an elected committee of workers he went in to see the management.

3rd May 1981, Bydgoszcz
Two days after the pathetic May Day parade in Warsaw, I watched
the crowd get bigger and bigger in Bydgoszcz. It spilled out of the
beautiful town square, over the bridge on the River Brda and into
the tiny streets around. More than 100,000 people, about half from
the important chemical and industrial works around Bydgoszcz and
about half from the newly formed Rural Solidarity, turned up to
celebrate the 190th anniversary of Poland's constitution. It was one
of Solidarity's biggest public demonstrations since the unveiling in
mid-December 1980, of the monuments to the workers killed in the
1970 Baltic Coast demonstrations.

Ask a German where Bydgoszcz is and he will scratch his head.
Mention Bromberg, the name by which it was known when part of
the Prussian, later the German, Empire from 1772 to 1919, and he
will place it instantly. German newspapers still refer to Danzig,
Breslau, Stettin rather than Gdansk, Wroclaw or Szczecin as they
are known in Polish. Over the centuries, the frontiers of Poland
have ebbed and flowed according to her power and position in the
always unsettled world between Berlin, Vienna and Moscow. Poles
will look back fondly to the 15th century when Poland stretched
from the Black Sea, taking in most of the Ukraine to what is nearly
its western frontier now. In 1920, the Red Army tried to export its
revolution at bayonet point into Poland, after the Poles had tried
to take advantage of Russia's weakness following 1917. The 1920
Battle (in Poland it is known as the Miracle) of the Vistula, threw
back the Red Army and a victorious Marshall Pilsudski laid claim
to much of what is now the Western Soviet Union, including Lvov
and Wilno. In 1945, in turn, Poland was given much of what had
previously been under German rule, including the rich industrial
and coal-heavy Upper Silesia.

The demography of all these areas has been largely altered by
massive population transfers following 1945. Young radical conservative Poles will openly talk of the territory that was part of Poland
1920-1939 as "under Russian occupation", while in the Federal
Republic of Germany, school maps are still issued showing chunks
of Western Poland as being within Germany's integral boundaries.
In Great Britain or the United States where settled frontiers have
been in existence for scores of generations, it may be difficult to imagine that political geography is more than the dullest subject in the
school syllabus. In Poland it is an important political reality, mix-
ing memories, fears and ambitions and conditioning both Solidarity's and the Polish government's handling of the complex problems
they have had to face since August 1980.

In the latter half of the 18th century and right up to 1919, Poland
did not exist as an independent State. It was partitioned three times

and divided up between Russia, Germany and Austria-Hungary. Each empire handled its portion of Poland in a different way. The Germans tried to fully incorporate Poland; the Russians forbade the Polish language to be used in schools; while the Austrians were more gentle, but offered no real freedom. The French Revolution temporarily shook loose the first tri-empire partition of Poland and on 3 May 1791, Poland's constitution was promulgated. It was a remarkably liberal document for its time: freeing serfs; giving civil rights to Jews and other minorities; and opening up elections to a much wider franchise.

The constitution, with its echoes of both the French and American revolutions was too much for Poland's imperial neighbours and although backed up by a military revolt in 1794, remained a glorious memory. Poland was partitioned for the third and final time in 1795. After Poland became an independent state in 1919, May 3rd was the national holiday, but this ceased after one-party rule was installed in 1947.

So, 1981 was the first year that the Poles openly celebrated May 3rd since before the war. Luckily it fell on a Sunday, so there was no problem about taking a day off. The government and party tried to organise its own festivities with cultural events in Warsaw, but it was the major Solidarity inspired celebrations that captured popular support. In Bydgoszcz, I listened in the middle of a packed crowd to a speech from the President of the Regional Solidarity, Jan Rulewski, which was followed by Mass. In the afternoon, miners' bands from Silesia gave open-air concerts, while families strolled about buying trinkets from peasants' stalls. In the municipal theatre, Polish dance groups performed. The city was smothered in posters reprinting the 1791 constitution and in particular, its three principles, two of which mirror those of the French revolution, and one which is distinctive — Liberty, Equality and Truth.

Two weeks before, a conference of teachers in Southern Poland had been informed by education ministry officials that the history textbooks used in schools and universities were to be altered so as to give more objective and adequate coverage to Polish pre-war history, the Stalin-Hitler non-aggression pact that carved up Poland in 1939, and the role of non-Communists in the fight against the Nazis during the war. The day after the May 3rd celebrations in Bydgoszcz, I attended a packed seminar in the press club in Warsaw. The lecture hall was jammed with journalists, teachers, university lecturers, listening to some of Poland's leading historians and political scientists debating the differences between Roman Dmowski and Jozef Pilsudski. Both men had dominated Polish politics in the inter-war years, Pilsudski, starting life, like

Mussolini, as a Socialist and ending up a militaristic, authoritarian dictator. With all Poland's problems in 1981 why were so many people engaged in passionate debate about two long-dead politicians whose ideas were reactionary enough, even in their own day? "You forget", I was told, "we have had no open political debate since 1947. Polish foreign defence and much of its internal policy has been dictated from outside. The development of political thought has been frozen for 40 years. That is why we plough over the past."

In the plant and regional bulletins produced by Solidarity there are many references to Poland's history. The history is not always so far in the distant past. Youngsters in Bydgoszcz had plastered the city with small posters and slogans reminding people of Katyn, the forest near Smolensk in which 4,000 Polish officers were killed by Stalin's NKVD after the Soviet occupation of Eastern Poland in 1939. The right-wing Confederation for an Independent Poland, whose leaders were imprisoned by September 1980, is based around the idea of national sovereignty and freedom from Russian domination.

To understand Solidarity, you have to take into account Polish history and what a powerful effect the sense of their own history, particularly the long struggle to win complete political, economic and cultural independence from more powerful neighbours, has for the Poles. It may seem strange that a workers' movement should boycott May Day and instead celebrate as its first national holiday a bourgeois document published two centuries ago. But, in a country where May Day had become a symbol of compulsion, not even the party leadership's decision to step down from the podium and join the parade could persuade Solidarity that May Day 1981 was a worker's event. Instead, workers invoked memories of past struggle and national achievement. They would wait until 31st August 1981, to commemorate the greatest victory in the history of the Polish working class — the signing of the Gdansk Agreement.

Chapter 2

Lech Walesa
and Solidarity's Leaders

At the end of 1980 newspaper editors all over the world were undecided about whom to nominate as Man of the Year. The choice lay between the 69-year-old actor just elected as President of the United States, or the 37-year-old Polish electrician who was leader of 10 million workers. For most Poles the answer was easy. Lech Walesa, in the space of three months, had become a hero for his own countrymen and a symbolic figure known all over the world. Walesa is of great importance to Solidarity, but the union is far from being a one-man show. All the major decisions taken by Solidarity are decided on a democratic, collective basis. The more powerful regional centres of Solidarity operate without reference to Walesa. There is an understandable resentment among some sections of Solidarity that the Western media pay too much attention to Walesa and ignore the other working-class leaders who play an equally important role in deciding Solidarity's policies and activities. To read much of the Western media's accounts of what has happened in Poland since August 1980, is to see everything in terms of Lech Walesa. He is portrayed as a kind of superman of East European free trade unionism and his social, economic and political roots are rarely adequately described, whilst the rest of Solidarity's leadership is left very much in the background.

Meeting Walesa

Lech Walesa's office is at the end of a corridor on the fifth floor of Solidarity's national headquarters in Gdansk. The national centre for Solidarity is a former seamen's hotel three miles from the shipyards and docks. The rooms are small, many of them still with washbasins in the corner. The building is grubby and even nine months after Solidarity's creation has a makeshift air. The growth of Solidarity and its rudimentary administration means that it is not yet possible to arrive at completely accurate figures of its total membership. Eight million is a conservative estimate; ten million a trifle generous. In this book I have played safe and put Solidarity's membership at 8-10 million. The office suite of the leader of 8-10 million trade unionists consists of two tiny rooms. In one sits his secretary, while Walesa's office is the size of seedy provincial hotel bedrooms all over the world. There is a wardrobe against the wall

on which is pinned a map of Poland. On another wall there is a
crucifix and a Polish eagle. A divan, an armchair, a small office
desk and two hard chairs make up the office furniture. Half-a-
dozen people in it make it appear crowded.

To get to Walesa is not very difficult. It you hang around the
Gdansk headquarters long enough he will appear. Instantly there is
a crowd around him: visitors with a problem, wellwishers who want
to shake his hand, an endless flow of journalists from the West
with questions to put. Everywhere Walesa goes he is accompanied
by a burly bodyguard cum assistant called Henryk. Henryk has the
size and weight and the sometimes friendly, sometimes unfriendly,
authority to protect Walesa from all those who want to stop him
for a second or two. I met Walesa first one late afternoon in mid-
December, 1980. He had been involved in long and tiring talks with
a government minister who had come to Gdansk to discuss
Solidarity's complaints about the provision of food for Christmas.
There was a long queue of people outside his office waiting to see
him. Luckily, I was with Ryszard Kalinowski, whom I had got to
know well as we travelled to Silesia to celebrate a miners' festival a
few days previously. Kalinowski is a Vice-President of Solidarity
and he was able to take me past the queue, brush aside the protests
of Henryk, and usher me into Walesa's office. Oh no, (I could see
the look in his eyes), not another foreigner to be polite to. He said
he was very tired, but Kalinowski asked him to spare a few minutes.
Walesa went over to the washbasin in the corner, splashed some
water in his face, combed his hair and stood up a new man, eager,
friendly and ready to talk.

The first thing that strikes you is that he is small, 5ft 7in with a
strong, stocky body. Newspaper and magazine photographs do
more than justice to his face, which is flat with a grey skin. The
moustache sweeps past the corners of his mouth, while his big
Polish nose and strong chin add an unmistakably Slavonic look. He
has the large, strong hands of a manual worker. Usually they are
holding a cigarette or a pipe. Walesa's incessant smoking is one of
his wife's biggest complaints.

He is usually dressed in a cheap suit or a denim jacket with an
open-necked shirt. In the cold winter months he wears a thick
parka. Now, in Poland, he is recognised everywhere. When in
Rome to see the Pope, he wanted to go for a walk with his wife.
"But", he added, "I would have to shave off my moustache first."
On his jacket lapel he sports a badge carrying the image of the
Black Madonna of Czestochowa. If you look at the photographs
taken with visitors in his office you will always see the crucifix and
the Polish eagle in the background. It is Walesa himself who stage
manages this. When I met him he suggested that we take a picture

of the two of us together and he took my arm and pulled me over to the wall so that the image of Christ and Nation should be behind us.

It is difficult to convey the exact conversational style that Walesa uses. It is friendly and direct. His reputation is founded on saying what he thinks and saying it honestly. Yet, at the same time, he is a master of necessary equivocation, deflecting questions about the political role of Solidarity, or fears of a Soviet intervention, with a skill that would do credit to a diplomat with a lifetime's experience in dodging difficult questions. He is welcoming and puts people at their ease. He picks up what is said to him and in his reply makes direct reference to his questioner's remarks. He makes you feel that what you have said is really interesting and important to him. It is a natural, unforced technique that means you leave his company liking him and feeling that you are his friend.

It is with fellow workers that Walesa really displays his gifts as a leader. He is a born speaker, an orator who knows how to move his audience, how to hold its attention and to get it to accept the message he is putting over. It is not always an easy task. More often than not Walesa has had to use his authority and gift as a speaker to tell workers what they would prefer not to hear: that they should return to work, that they should act cautiously and that a specific demand would have to wait a little longer. In the winter of 1981, Walesa was driven into a state of near exhaustion as he travelled all over Poland, slowing down and calming the urge for swifter change and more action that many groups of workers were expressing. His style of oratory is not that of the loud, booming voice, the heavily worked images, or the peroration delivered with the arm-waving vigour of a Michael Foot or Ted Kennedy. He speaks quietly, talking in a friendly, direct way with the audience, no matter what its size. He talks about their daily experiences, their problems and what their new union is doing to solve them. He speaks, like all the best orators, without notes. The only recorded instance of his delivering a speech from a text was at a ceremony to inaugurate the memorial to the workers killed in Gdansk in 1970. Pope John Paul II noted this when they met at the Vatican in January 1981. After Walesa had said a few words the Pope got up to reply and remarked: "Mr Walesa is a young man and can speak without notes. However, at my age, I have to work from a prepared script."

He is also a good negotiator. The exchanges between Walesa (and other Solidarity representatives) and the government team led by Vice-Premier Mieczyslaw Jagielski during the Gdansk strike belong to the classic literature of worker-employer discussions. After a polite welcome from Walesa, Jagielski says; "These strikes must be terminated." Walesa replies: "They should have been stopped a long time ago, but we have been waiting for you. What is your position on our twenty-one claims?''

Jagielski replies with a phrase that every trade union negotiator has heard at the beginning of a negotiation from the lips of the employer's representative: "Allow me to begin by making some general points . . ." Walesa cuts in sharply. "No. I want a concrete answer, point by point." The exchange was conveyed on loudspeakers to the workers waiting anxiously outside. They exploded with pleasure. At long last they had a spokesman who would slice into the evasiveness of the government-employer. Walesa's insistence during the August negotiations on keeping Jagielski strictly to the point and obliging the government side to negotiate in specific detail was one of his major contributions to the success of the strike.

Walesa's Background

On 24th August 1980 there was a crisis meeting in Warsaw of Poland's rulers. Edward Gierek had finally realised the seriousness of the situation and returned from his holiday in the Crimea. Someone was explaining Walesa's power and hold over the striking workers. Gierek looked up and asked: "Can anyone tell me who this guy is?"

Walesa was born on 29th September 1943, in the small village of Popow between Warsaw and Gdansk. He was the fourth child in a poor family struggling under the Nazi occupation. His father died in 1945 and Leszek (the diminutive is Lech) grew up in a Poland devastated by the war. Between 1939 and 1945 six million Polish citizens, nearly a fifth of the country's population, had been killed. 38 per cent of the country's industrial capacity had been destroyed, as had 35 per cent of its agricultural resources. 30 per cent of Poland's housing stock and 60 per cent of its schools were razed as Soviet and German armies turned Poland into the fighting ground on which the outcome of the war depended. (At a press conference in Warsaw a Russian journalist from TASS complained bitterly about his Western confreres asking endless questions about the arrival of Soviet troops in Poland. "Everyone knows," he said, "that there are already 600,000 Russian soldiers on Polish soil." "Oh no we don't," said the Western journalists, "where are they?" "They left their bodies here to liberate Poland from the Nazis," was the TASS man's lofty reply).

After the war the Communists placed great emphasis on schooling. Many of Solidarity's leaders, still aged only in their twenties and thirties, have had very good schooling that lasted until they were sixteen or eighteen, even though they were not going on to follow higher education. If one discounts the compulsory Russian courses, the Stalinist line and the distortions in history, post-war education in Poland does great credit to the country. From the point of view of some, it may all have been a great mistake, for Poland's schools have produced a generation of workers much better equipped to question and challenge the organisation of economic and social relations in the country.

From the age of seven Walesa attended a school at Chalin, two miles from Popow, staying there until he was fourteen. This was followed by two years at a technical school. In 1959 he began work as an electrician in the repair shop of an agricultural co-operative. A few years later he moved to Gdansk for the better paid post of an electrician in the shipyards and to get away from the tiny, enclosed world of peasant Poland.

In 1969 he married a florist, Danuta. They have six children. The youngest, Anna, was born at 3 a.m. on 2nd August 1980. Her father was released from prison at 10 a.m. the same day. He had been arrested for distributing leaflets urging support for the strikes then hitting Poland. Their life was simple and hard. They got up at 6 a.m. and had breakfast followed by Mass. Walesa would take his sandwiches to work, (work that became more intermittent and difficult to obtain after he was sacked from the Lenin Shipyards in 1976) and come home in mid-afternoon at the end of his shift for the principal meal of the day. There were no holidays and great difficulty in making ends meet for the growing family. It was only in September 1980 that they moved from their two-room apartment to a bigger apartment. Now he has a monthly salary of 7,000 zlotys ($205, £85) from Solidarity. Much as Walesa is an easy mixer and gets on well with everyone he meets, he had the reputation during the 1970s of being something of a loner. At meetings of the activists who formed Free Trade Union of the Coast he would sit quietly at the back of the room soaking up the discussion and arguments and not attempting to impose his own personality. In the many millions of words written about Walesa and the scores of thousands spoken by him to journalists since August 1980, it is impossible to find a coherent political or trade union theory which either explains his actions or provides definite clues to his future behaviour. A group of miners in Silesia asked him who could teach them democracy. He replied: "Who? Not Leszek, for he is too small, too stupid. Yourselves. Everybody." Perhaps the best Western comparison is with a tough shop steward or local branch chairman in a union organising skilled workers: someone who is never afraid to take on management, skilled at talking to his members, with a proven record of sacrifice and struggle, yet someone who is never 100 per cent predictable for either his members or for the employers. This last quality is important for Walesa. Like most workers, he

distrusts intellectuals and in many interviews has spoken of them
disparagingly. He has to listen to the advice of very many intellectuals, however, and decide which conflicting advice to follow.
Neither Solidarity nor the government is ever sure which way
Walesa will go and it, therefore, makes no sense to argue, as some
Western commentators have done, that Walesa is in the hands of
any particular group — Church, KOR or the Catholic intelligentsia. Although a devout Catholic, and there can be no doubt that
Walesa's completely unshakeable faith in Catholicism provides him
with a self-confidence, he will not necessarily allow the Church to
tell him what to do. In the Gdansk strike he ignored the clear
message from the late Cardinal Wyszinski to call off the strike.

But he can also be flexible. Two days into the Gdansk strike the
local management had conceded the strikers' demands for the
reinstatement of Anna Walentynowicz and a big wage rise. They
had shuffled off the other demands to further talks and Walesa was
ready to leave it at that. While workers were considering what to
do, a young woman worker took the microphone and pointed out
that many other factories were also on strike in the Gdansk region.
If Walesa allowed the Lenin Shipyard workers to go back then the
other strikes would be severely weakened. The crowd of workers
murmured approval and Walesa at once changed tack and said that
although the reinstatement/wage rise strike was over they would
continue to occupy the yard in order to obtain satisfaction in
respect of their other demands and for the rest of the region's
strikers.

Towards the end of the Gdansk negotiations, when the Government had conceded the 21 points, Walesa was ready to sign. One
problem was in the way. The government had arrested Jacek
Kuron, Adam Michnik and other KOR activists and was holding
them in prison. Many of the delegates had said that release of the
prisoners should be a pre-condition for the signing of the agreement and the end of the strike. The advisers and experts surrounding Walesa at the time were mainly the intellectuals associated
with the Club for the Catholic Intelligentsia in Warsaw. They
argued, on the other hand, that it would be a mistake to jeopardise
the tremendous advances contained in the agreement which the
government was ready to sign, for the sake of getting, prior to
signature, the release of Kuron and other KOR people who would
almost certainly be released in any case once the strike was over. It
is probable that this view was shared by Walesa. But, like a skilful
working-class leader, he knew that whatever his own inclination, to
leave Kuron and the others in prison would dismay the delegates
assembled from striking plants all over the region and would end
the strike on a rancorous note. Brilliantly he turned the issue

round, putting the pressure on Jagielski to avoid a breakdown of the negotiations because of a government insistence on Kuron's continued imprisonment. To the Catholic intellectuals it seemed a risky gamble. Walesa intuitively felt that with the strike getting stronger, and with more support being announced from other parts of Poland every hour, it was the workers that could successfully afford not to compromise.

Critics of Walesa inside Solidarity point to the episode as an example of Walesa's vacillation. From a simplistic point of view it is an accurate criticism, but it ignores the need for flexibility, essential in any trade union leader. A rigidly moderate or rigidly militant leader of Solidarity would be disastrous for Poland's workers. Walesa's fly-by-the-seat-of-his-pants technique of leadership may not be sufficient for all time, but since August 1980 it has most certainly been necessary for the Polish working class.

Even Walesa's harshest critics — be they workers or intellectuals — admit that he is indispensable. Poland has not had a national hero since the death in 1935 of Marshall Pilsudski. Now it has two — the Pope and Lech Walesa. In almost any circle or group of people you have just to pronounce his name (in Polish the 'l' in Walesa is not the English ell sound, but a 'w' while the 'e' has an accent attached to it which strongly nasalises the vowel, so the correct pronunciation is *Vaawensa)* and there is immediate interest in what he is like, what he has been saying or doing. For the first time since the war the Poles have a national leader whose word they trust. Even if some may not like what he says, they know he is speaking sincerely and honestly.

One does not have to hold traditional views of national history to acknowledge the importance of the role of heroes. Walesa's development and future behaviour will be of the utmost importance for Solidarity. His idiosyncratic style may not fit in so easily with a more institutionalised Solidarity whose leadership is based on formal statutory elections rather than the spontaneous *ad hoc* leadership thrown up in the Autumn of 1980. He has given gentle hints that he sees himself as a kind of general leader not tied down to day-to-day chairing of meetings or administration.

Solidarity's Leadership

But, important as Walesa may be, Solidarity is far from being his fief — its decisions are taken on a collective basis. Moreover, its strong regional organisation means that many decisions are taken on the spot without reference back to the national headquarters in Gdansk. Solidarity's leaders, as they emerged in the Autumn of 1980, were nearly all children of Communist Poland. Their age spread is from 25 to 45, with a majority in the late 20's or 30's.

Most are skilled workers, married with families. Bogdan Lis, 28, was a labourer at the Elmor electrical works in Gdansk. He is a Communist Party member and was vice-chairman of the Union of Young Socialists in his factory. He was elected to the praesidium of the Inter-Factory strike committee in Gdansk in August 1980, and quickly became one of the top leaders of national Solidarity. Ryszard Kalinowski, also 28, is head of Solidarity at Elblag, 45 miles from Gdansk. He is a skilled turner and is now responsible for international relations on Solidarity's national committee. The chairman of the 750,000-strong Cracow Region is a 36-year-old steelworker, Mieczyslaw Gil.

The chairman of Solidarity in Radom, scene of the 1976 workers' strike is a 31-year-old metalworker, Andrzej Sobieraj, while the chairman of Solidarity's biggest region, the Mazowsze region, which includes Warsaw and seven surrounding Voivodships (regional districts) is a 26-year-old tractor factory worker, Zbigniew Bujak. In Bydgoczsz, one of Poland's major industrial and chemical centres, the chairman of Solidarity is a 34-year-old machinist, Jan Rulewski.

Two important figures in Solidarity, Marian Jurczyk of Szczecin and Andrzej Gwiazda of Gdansk are older, both in their mid-40's and are white-collar technical workers. Each represents a different tendency inside the union. Gwiazda was one of the principal founders and the main ideological driving force behind the Free Trade Union of the Baltic Coast. Bearded, and dressed casually in corduroy trousers and a sweater, he speaks with great intensity and there are relatively few religious or nationalist references in his interviews and speeches. Although Walesa received all the international publicity, it was Gwiazda who played an equally, some say more, important role in the Gdansk negotiations, by his insistence on making the creation of independent trade unions the very centre of the dispute.

He also wrote into Solidarity's statutes the right of members to recall delegates. He has quarrelled badly with Walesa, particularly over the latter's behaviour during the decision to call off the national strike threatened over the beating up of Solidarity leaders in Bydgoszcz in March 1981. Gwiazda represents the ultra-democratic, and uncompromising wing of Solidarity. Trade union tradition has it that the purists gradually get squeezed out of the top leadership of any union organisation. Their uncompromising style does not fit into the pattern of what a former General Secretary of the TUC called "the shoddy, shabby compromises" that trade unions have to make. When I first visited the Solidarity national headquarters in Gdansk in 1980, Gwiazda's office was just beside Walesa's. Re-visiting Gdansk in the Summer of 1981, I noticed that his office, while still on the all-important fifth floor, had been moved to the other end of the long, long corridor and was now well away from Walesa's.

Marian Jurczyk, chairman of Solidarity in Szczecin, could not be more different. Clean shaven, he is always neatly dressed in a suit. He is a draughtsman who has established good relations with the party and regional authorities in Szczecin. When asked what Solidarity's major achievement had been, he told me it was to get Sunday Mass broadcast on the radio. He talks optimistically about putting the right kind of Pole into the government and his conversation is scattered with references to the Church and Nation. He says that Poland should become a country whose culture and sense of patriotism sets an example to other countries. By any Western standards Jurczyk is a cautious trade union moderate. Yet, he has created a sufficient margin of operation in Szczecin to have persuaded the authorities to permit the printing on State presses of Solidarity's most lively journal *Jednosc*, which often carries much of the controversial debate inside the union, including details of Gwiazda's disagreements with Walesa.

The nature of Solidarity's leadership may well change as a result of formal elections and that process is discussed below. The position of Walesa will continue to be extremely significant. But he will remain under the control of a collective leadership which will be firmly rooted in the working class. But, there is one glaring absence from the leadership of Solidarity at both national and regional level, that of women. Apart from Anna Walentynowicz and Alina Pienkowska, a nurse in the medical centre in the Lenin Shipyard, who are active in Gdansk, there is only one woman member of the national leadership of Solidarity. Women rarely figure in the regional leaderships. At an electric fittings factory near Wroclaw, where three quarters of the workforce are female, there were only six women among the 66 candidates who offered themselves for election for the Solidarity plant committee. The leadership of Solidarity remains very much a man's affair.

Chapter 3

The Road to Gdansk

Marian Jurczyk was smiling. He had just received the new flag for Pomeranian Solidarity of which he was President. In his spacious office in Szczecin he wanted to show off his latest pride and joy and I was to have the honour of being the first outside visitor to see it. I have marched behind many different banners in labour movement demonstrations, but have never seen one on which so much love and skill had been lavished. It was fringed with rich gold tassels. One side simply bore the name Solidarnosc (Solidarity), red on white, while the other had the Polish eagle with the image of the Black Virgin of Czestochowa sewn into the centre of the flag. Visually it was another reminder of the Catholic-Nationalist symbolism so strong in Solidarity. But around the eagle in a sparkling gold on mauve background were five dates: 1956, 1968, 1970, 1976 and 1980. Three of those dates represent a workers' revolt which was bloodily put down by the authorities, one a students' uprising that was to have important effects for intellectuals' links with workers, and the last, 1980, the year of the Gdansk Agreement (though in Szczecin they are a little tired of the obsessive focus on Gdansk and point out to visitors that in the Szczecin shipyard, workers and others were also on strike in the second half of August 1980 and in their negotiations with a government minister secured concessions broadly similar to those agreed in Gdansk).

In the early 1970's the following joke was widespread in Poland: *Question:* What is the difference between Edward Gierek and Wladyslaw Gomulka? (Gierek's predecessor as First Secretary 1956-1970). *Answer:* There is no difference, only Gierek does not yet realise it!

Three times since the war revolt by workers has forced the resignation of Poland's leader. According to Edmund Baluka, leader of the Szcecin metalworkers in 1970, Polish workers learned from their experiences of 1956, 1970 and 1976 — without having gone through those struggles and defeats the victory of 1980 would not have been possible.

1956

From the moment the country was liberated by the Red Army in 1945, Poland's Communist leaders followed a political and economic line laid down by Moscow. The older generation of Communist leaders had been killed in Moscow during Stalin's 1938 purge. Rosa Luxembourg, perhaps the greatest Polish Marxist, whose theories of proletarian internationalism and workers' control could have made a useful theoretical contribution to the development of Polish Communism, was, of course, on a blacklist, her books and ideas unavailable anywhere in Eastern Europe. Poland, like other East European countries, was obliged to adopt a programme of heavy industrialisation after the war, with highly centralised planning, norms that factory managers were expected to meet, and, all of this backed up by a secret police, the UB (later to change its initials to SB).

Polish trade unions followed the Soviet model, which was imposed all over Eastern Europe — a national trade union centre (CRZZ) with industrial sections for metalworkers, printers, railwaymen, etc. Union officials were appointed by the party and busied themselves with organising social facilities, sports fields, holiday camps and minor personnel matters. In no way did they press economic or political demands. The key function of these officials was, in fact, to ensure disciplined labour organisation. To some extent it worked. Between 1950 and 1955, according to official figures, the index of producer goods went up three times, while non-agricultural employment went up by 60 per cent. Before 1939 two in three Poles depended on the land. By 1980 the agricultural workforce was down to six million out of a total population of 36 million. From being a relatively backward peasant country Poland became, by the end of the 1970's, the world's eleventh industrial power. This process changed the distribution of the country's adult population. It became an industrialised, urbanised working class.

Although Poland's leaders avoided the worst excesses of Stalinism — there were no show trials in the early 1950's for Communist Party leaders, as in Czechoslovakia, for example — the party, about one million strong in 1953, found it hard to cope with the events that followed Stalin's death in 1953, and the consequent and confusing changes in direction from Moscow.

A certain liberalisation unfolded. Wladyslaw Gomulka, the Party's First Secretary after the war, who had been imprisoned in 1949 because of his advocacy of a national Communism within Poland, was released. Writers and intellectuals started to speak up. The student newspaper *Po Prostu* declared in 1955: "We are people who cannot stop meddling with all that happens around us. We are a group of discontented; we want more things, better things, wiser things".

Workers shared that desire. Very little had been done to raise workers' living standards. Consumer goods were not being produced. Social and medical services had a low priority. In June 1956, workers at ZISPO engineering plant in Poznan went on strike. Quickly their call went beyond economic benefits and extended to political freedoms.

Like most workers who want to make a point beyond stopping work they decided to organise a march through the city. The Polish Secret Police was waiting and opened fire. Fifty workers were killed and several hundred wounded.* The revolt may have been put down, but it signalled a major change for the Polish Communist Party. For the rest of the Summer of 1956 an intense internal debate took place, not unlike the kind of debate inside the Party since August 1980. The news of Krushchev's denunciation of Stalin's crimes and the invasion of Hungary added to the re-thinking about the nature of the Communist Party inside Poland. The first encouraged the liberal reformers, while the Russian tanks in Budapest reminded everyone of the limits in political relaxation that would be permitted.

Following Poznan, workers set up workers' councils in many factories, parallel to the official unions, to act as representatives of workers' grievances and to put pressure on factory managements to operate more effectively.

Strikes and workplace protests continued throughout the Autumn of 1956. The political problem was resolved by the election of Gomulka as First Secretary at a Party Central Committee meeting in October 1956. Gomulka promised decentralised management and planning, a real voice for workers, including recognition of workers' councils and he attacked the economic policies followed since 1949. At the same time, while stressing the need for equality in Polish-Soviet relations, he declared that he would not pursue an anti-Soviet policy. It was a convincing policy (the policy and the period of liberalisation around it later became known as the Polish October) that defused the tension running through Poland since the Poznan workers had been repressed. But the expectations were not to be met. The ideas of the intellectuals for increasing autonomy for courts, parliament, professional groups, as well as liberalisation of cultural and religious practices was of little interest to Gomulka. Intellectuals, he said, are people "who produce neither steel nor bread, but only chit-chat". Nor did he push for economic reforms which would have transformed the economy. In May 1957, Poland's Economic Advisory Council urged that individual enterprises should be given greater autonomy,

---

* The Politburo member sent to investigate the handling of the Poznan revolt was Edward Gierek. He was critical of the UB handling of the demonstrators and a stock of batons were hurriedly imported from West Germany so that small arms would not, in the first instance, need to be used.

with control of wages and prices de-centralised. Workers' councils should run enterprises jointly with a State-appointed director. The object in the words of *Po Prostu* "was to bring about a radical transformation of the Stalinist model of Socialism to a Polish model, genuinely Socialist".

It was all too much for Gomulka. An old style Communist, he believed that only a centrally controlled, one-party State guaranteed Socialism. Liberalise the economy, allow workers to dismiss managers and ignore party directives, permit intellectuals to say and write what they pleased and where would it all end? In October 1957 he was accusing the liberalisers of the worst sin in Marxism-Leninism. They were, he said, "revisionists". They were worse than the Stalinists, he told the Central Committee, because they were like tuberculosis: whilst the Stalinists were akin to influenza. "Influenza, even in its most serious form, cannot be cured by contracting tuberculosis. Dogmatism cannot be cured by revisionism. Revisionist tuberculosis can only strengthen dogmatic influenza. The revisionist", he concluded, "must be expelled from the Party".

It was the end of the Polish October. Centralised planning was firmed up. *Po Prostu* was closed down. Protesting students were beaten up by special militia squads, set up following Gierek's investigation into the Poznan revolt. The workers' councils were incorporated into the official unions. Lechoslaw Gozdzik, the workers' leader at the FSO automobile factory in Warsaw, was fired.

Although collective farms were broken up and returned to private ownership, Gomulka could develop no settled policy for Polish agriculture. Relationships with the Catholic Church were eased, but the power and budget of the security police increased. Workers saw their hopes of reforms based on remaining within the one-party system crumble away.

1968

There were very few instances of workers' fight-back against the State or Party in the years that followed the collapse of the Polish October. Workers such as Anna Walentynowicz, who tried in the 1960s to raise questions such as the mis-use of trade union subscriptions by senior officers of the official trade unions, found themselves transferred to less well paid jobs in the Lenin Shipyard at Gdansk. Instead, the opposition to Gomulka came from intellectuals and students. In 1964, Jacek Kuron and Karol Modzielewski published their "Open Letter to the Communist Party". It was a reasoned critique that blamed the all-powerful bureaucracy for deforming Socialism, and accused the State of betraying the workers' interests. The State's response to such left-wing criticism was to dismiss both men from their posts as junior lecturers at Warsaw University. They were arrested and given two-year prison sentences in 1965.

Before the war Poland had many anti-semitic tendencies. Polish Jews were strongly ghettoised and in the 1930's the army-dominated Polish government turned a blind eye to attacks on Jews. Many of Poland's leading Communists, who had spent the war in the Soviet Union, were of Jewish origin. As the continued fight for control of the party developed during the 1960's, an anti-semitic wing rose around General Mieczyslaw Moczar, Polish Minister of the Interior and leader of the powerful veterans' organisation. The Israeli-Arab Six-Day War in 1967 unleashed a wave of anti-Israeli, anti-Zionist propaganda inside Eastern Europe. In Poland, Communist Jews were forced out of their jobs. Adam Rapacki, Poland's distinguished Foreign Minister, was handed a list of 40 Jews he was expected to purge from his ministry. Rapacki, although not Jewish, added his own name to the top of the list as a protest, and disappeared into retirement. Party hardliners seized the opportunity to force out of office reformist party members who were not Jewish. It was to be the final settling of accounts with those who supported the Polish October.

Mixed up with the anti-Jewish campaign was a crackdown against students and intellectuals who, in March 1968, had raised demands for greater intellectual freedom. A demonstration organised in protest against the authorities' banning of a classical Polish play which contained some anti-Russian remarks was savagely put down by Moczar. Hundreds of students were expelled from university, and many lecturers lost their jobs. The influence of the Prague Spring was important. A popular slogan said: "Poland is waiting for its Dubcek".

The repression, which by now mixed up Jews and non-Jews, continued. Nine thousand people lost their positions, including senior party members such as the secretary of the Central Committee and the editor of the Party newspaper, *Trybuna Ludu*. Ninety-nine Warsaw University lecturers were dismissed. Kuron, who is not Jewish, and Modzelewski, who is Jewish, and stepson of an important figure in the post-war Communist Party, were re-arrested and sentenced to three-and-a-half years in prison for participating in, and acting as "spiritual instigators" of, the student demonstrations. Upon their release they went their separate ways. Modzelewski became a medieval historian at Wroclaw University, while Kuron, unable to find a job, turned into a key oppositionist whose ideas, and, in particular, whose commitment to making contact and co-operating closely with workers, were to be of crucial importance in the late 1970's and in the events leading up to the Gdansk strike and agreement. Modzelewski emerged from academic seclusion in September 1980, to become Solidarity's national press spokesman and one of its most trusted advisers, though in March 1980, he gave up the position to return to Wroclaw, following a disagreement with Lech Walesa over the method of calling off a threatened national strike.

About 30,000 people, mainly Jewish, left Poland for exile in Western Europe, North America and Israel. A handful of Jews and non-Jewish intellectuals, newly arrived in exile, became a *de facto* network of Polish Socialist activists who would maintain contacts with Poland and the opposition that remained inside. They would provide money, help with printing equipment, arrange for material written in Poland to be published in the West. They would brief foreign journalists, trade unionists and politicians on what was happening inside Poland beyond the publicly available facts. Unlike the generation of Poles who went into exile as a result of World War II, the 1968 generation eschewed jejune anti-Communist propaganda and sought to persuade left-wing and trade union activists in the West of the importance of what was happening beneath the facade of settled Communist rule in Poland. Moczar's 1968 expulsions were to provide Poland with an important set of links with Western Socialists which no other East European country, except for Czechoslovakia, enjoys.

On the surface things had settled down by the end of 1969. There had been no public protest against the jail sentences of those arrested after the Warsaw riots. One of the most bizarre forms of opposition came from Albania, where Kazimierz Mijal, a former member of the Polish Central Committee had defected in 1966. Broadcasting on Radio Tirana in Polish, he denounced the "counter-revolutionary Gomulka clique". In Warsaw, the Polish police organised a pro-Soviet demonstration outside the Chinese Embassy and banned the import of Chairman Mao's little red book. In retaliation the Chinese invited selected oppositionists to a showing inside the embassy of films which claimed to prove the guilt of the Soviet Union in the Katyn massacre of Polish officers.

1970

Fourteen years after the Poznan workers' uprising, and the Polish October, Gomulka had failed to improve the lot of the working class. The percentage of the gross national product invested in heavy industry rose from 24.2 per cent in 1960 to 29.7 per cent in 1969. There was a neglect of consumer goods, housing and services. Above all, agriculture lagged behind inefficiently. Low State

prices, difficulties in obtaining agricultural machinery and fer-
tilizers, and compulsory delivery of certain produce, gave no encouragement to the peasants to produce more efficiently. A
worsening trade deficit meant that the export of agricultural produce, and in particular, meat had to be stepped up. Pork, which in
the form of ham and sausage is central to Polish diet, was in very
short supply.

Some commentators have been too harsh on Gomulka's
economic policies. To wrench Poland out of its agricultural
backwardness and wartime destruction and make it an industrial
power is not a task that could easily be achieved, while
simultaneously maintaining social harmony. Capitalist states in
South America and Asia have made similar economic transitions in
recent years, and always at the cost of denying political, trade
union and human rights. In Poland, however, there were no
multinational corporations or interfering foreign ambassadors to
blame. The Party controlled the country. The Party claimed credit
for Poland's successes. It was therefore, the Party that the workers
accused of economic mismanagement when the rising expectations
of workers failed to be met. By the late 1960's workers were suffering a stagnation in their standard of living. Although there were
some wage increases, these were quickly soaked up.

Formal prices mean relatively little in Poland. Although public
housing is cheap, there are waiting lists of up to 20 years to get a
small family apartment. The existence of a widespread and
tolerated black market, in which goods (including food) not
available in the shops can be bought at high prices, means that a
much higher proportion of an average Polish family's income is used for food and essential household purchases than a simple comparison between wages and official prices would indicate.

Gomulka's decision to push through food price increases, including a 30 per cent rise in meat prices in 1970, provoked workers'
protests in the Baltic ports of Gdansk, Gdynia and Szczecin. The
protests took the form of a work stoppage coupled with disorganis-
ed forays into the streets. In Szczecin, workers burnt down the Party headquarters. Conflicting accounts describe the specific repression of the strikes. Lech Walesa, then a 27-year-old Lenin Shipyard
worker in Gdansk, described it this way. "The dawn of 16th
December 1970, tanks were placed in front of Gate No. 2 of the
shipyard. People were frightened and did not know what to do.
They started to disperse and leave the yard. I could not, or did not
know how to, convince them that they must stay behind barricades
inside the yard. Some provocative elements started to throw things,
to burn things down and tried to break into the Party headquarters.
Then the militia opened fire." Officially the death toll was 45 in

Gdansk and about the same in Szczecin, where the army had told workers it was safe to leave the yard and then opened fire. In Szczecin, however they say that 200 workers were killed.

The Baltic massacres were responsible for the fall of Gomulka, who was replaced on 19th December 1970 by the Party Secretary of the Silesian region, Edward Gierek; but this did not stop the strikes. Gierek was forced to go in person to both Gdansk and Szczecin and, with a 25 per cent wage increase, he persuaded workers to return. In mid-February 1971 there was a wave of strikes in Lodz and the government announced that the food price rises would be cancelled.

The slaughter of the Baltic Coast strikers was to be bitterly remembered all through the 1970's. Ten years is not so long in a worker's lifetime. Although they had no outstanding leaders and were relatively unorganised, workers had demonstrated that they could win wage increases, cancel price rises and remove the leader of a one-party State. After the dead years between 1956 and 1970 it was a demonstration of workers' power, even if the price in lives lost was high. And from 1970 the workers of the Baltic would draw important lessons for 1980.

Nor did workers' militancy die with the wage increases, price annulments and the arrival of Gierek in power. In Szczecin they elected Edmund Baluka, one of the 1970 strike leaders, as President of the regional branch of the official metalworkers' union. Commenting on the 1970 strikes, Baluka said, "We now know how to go on strike. We don't know how to win a strike". The official union had been thrown by the Szczecin massacres, but judged it better to have an authentic workers' representative in, at least, an important figurehead position. In October 1972 Baluka found himself to be the sole delegate among the 2,800 assembled for the metalworkers' congress who voted against the official policy resolution. "When I made my intervention, one of my demands was for the complete independence of unions from the Party. Unfortunately, the next speaker was Gierek, who said firmly that Party and unions must stay together." On his return to Szczecin, Baluka was removed from his official union post and sacked from his shipyard job.

In early 1973, the authorities made it possible for him to slip onto a ship that was leaving Poland. He worked for nearly three years as a fitter in Liverpool and Manchester, and then edited, in Polish, a Trotskyist newspaper in Paris. Baluka tried to get the paper, called *The Gadfly,* circulated inside Poland, but its caustic anti-religious tone did not go down well with workers. In April 1981, Baluka re-entered Poland on false papers and, on Solidarity's advice, submitted his case to the public prosecutor.

The importance of Baluka is not his activity in exile, but the continued presence of an independent worker representing other workers in the period after the military repression of the 1970 food price rise strikes. The active Soviet policy of détente in this period, including the Helsinki Agreement by which Mr Brezhnev set such score, meant that the more cruel forms of repression and victimisation against individual militants could not be so easily practised.

In 1978, when President of the British National Union of Journalists, I visited the Czechoslovakian Union of Journalists in Prague and protested about the political victimisation of journalists who had been unable to work since 1969. "Listen, my friend," my opposite number said, "twenty-five years ago these people would have been tried and shot. Fifteen years ago they would have been put in prison. Now they simply lose their jobs. That's progress under Socialism." The cynicism contains an important point: despite the unpleasant and unacceptable victimisation of dissidents in Eastern Europe, and the Soviet Union's use of psychiatric hospitals to imprison oppositionists, the show trials followed by death sentences, the secret executions, and the widespread use of direct physical torture, belong to the past. There are limits to permitted repression.

In Poland the pattern of protest continued in the early 1970's. In 1974 dockyard workers struck in Gdynia. Silesian miners gained pay increases of 42 per cent in 1974 as the authorities tried to buy off potential militancy.

1976

The 1970s was a decade of extraordinary economic, as well as political, change in Poland. The arrival in power of Edward Gierek, the technological and consumption orientated leader from Silesia, saw a massive investment in heavy industry in Poland. Half of Poland's capital has been formed since 1970, most of it in the shape of massive loans from the West. By 1981 Poland owed $27 billion to the West and it was thought that the total value of Poland's exports to the West in 1981 would not fully cover her interest payments on this massive debt. In 1971, the Soviet Union lent Poland $100 million, in 1976 $1.3 billion and late in 1980 $1.35 billion. This massive indebtedness has clear implications for Western policy, as well as being an important factor in Russia's handling of the situation. However, to get the debt in perspective, it should be remembered that at the end of 1979 Yugoslavia had a foreign debt of $15 billion, almost twice the per-capita debt of Poland. In the early 1970's foreign money, especially from US banks, flowed into Poland, partly under the influence of détente policies. There was a massive rise in central investments — 7 per cent in 1971, 23 per cent in 1972, 25 per cent in 1973. Even after the 1973 oil price rise, investment in Poland continued at a high level.

Money wages also rose quickly — by 45 per cent between 1971 and 1976. Although there was a heavy increase in the production of consumer goods, cars and television sets, there were still massive shortages. This produced a black market for the middle classes and for those with privileged access to such purchases by virtue of jobs held or Party membership. But the working class was left out of this consumer boom. The use to which the loans were put was never effectively controlled by the lenders, and millions were wasted on buying equipment which could not be used, or were diverted into building luxurious offices for the Party or security police; and even into building dachas for regional officials.

In 1976 Gierek tried to go into reverse, with a slowing down of heavy industrial investment and a further increase in the production of consumer goods. But, as he tried to juggle with the economy, one figure stared from the balance sheet. The State was having to spend 12 per cent of its gross domestic product on supporting food prices. Gierek decided to plunge into the deep end with an increase in food prices of 60 per cent, announced for 1st July 1976.

In response there was a wave of sit-down strikes all over Poland, especially in Warsaw and the Baltic ports. In Radom, workers at an armaments factory stopped work and demonstrated against the price rises. In the Ursus tractor factory, the railway line which runs through the factory, connecting the capital to the west of Poland, was ripped up. The strike worked. Within two days the Polish Prime Minister was on television announcing the withdrawal of the price increases. But the repression was heavy. "Ring leaders" were sacked. Other workers involved were forced to run the gauntlet of militia men. In Radom there were reports of physical torture being used against strike leaders and prison sentences of twelve years were handed out. In December 1980 one of them told me that he did not worry whether or not the police knew he was active in Solidarity because they had all their names and photographs from 1976.

The important thing, however, is that the workers had shown consistently since 1970 that they had the power to defend their living standards, by stopping price rises or by gaining wage increases. Shooting them or sacking them in one place no longer stopped strikes elsewhere. Faced with workers' power, the government had no easy answer. However, feeling discontented, and going on strike against food prices is not enough. From 1976 the Polish workers introduced two new elements into the equation: organisation and politics.

Chapter 4

KOR,
the Growth of Free Unions
and the Crisis of 1980

The basement hall in Gdansk where Solidarity holds its national committee meetings is far from the comfortable, well decorated conference chambers provided for the national leaderships of the big unions and federations in other East European countries. It is a former hotel ballroom, with a small stage and rows of chairs on which sit the delegates representing the different regional centres of Solidarity. I arrived in mid-afternoon in December 1980, to find the morning session of the national committee on the point of breaking up.

Over lunch with Andrzej Gwiazda, Solidarity's Vice-President, and Jacek Kuron, a founder of KOR and the Soviet Union's public enemy number one in Poland, we talked about the problems then facing Solidarity. It was the height of a Soviet invasion scare and even President Carter had announced that the White House considered a Soviet invasion strongly possible. Kuron was angry with what he considered to be irresponsible reporting in the Western media: "We are extremely angry about the Western press that describes the situation here as one of panic. The people here in Poland, which is supposedly in danger, are quite calm".

As we talked, Kuron deferred continually to Gwiazda, insisting that I should talk to him about Solidarity's problems and policies. Like the other intellectuals and experts connected with Solidarity, Kuron was conscious that his role was to advise, not to lead; to suggest, not to order. He glides in and out of Solidarity meetings, his gruff voice picking up points and clarifying issues. Squat, bald, ugly, but with an attractive personality (he reminded me in physical stature of early photographs of Lord Beaverbrook) and usually dressed in jeans, an open-necked shirt and tartan lumber jacket, Kuron has, as often as not, acted as a moderating force on Solidarity since August 1980. But his role, and that of KOR, was crucial in the years between 1976 and 1980.

In the middle of May 1981, Moscow's influential *Literary Gazette* published two long articles on what was happening in Poland by Felix Kouznetsov, secretary of the Moscow Writers' Union. According to Mr Kouznetsov, KOR advocated a new type of socialism, a socialism "naturally without communists, without a leading role for the party, a Polish socialism, pluralist, national and with a human face". But, he went on to argue, the real object of KOR's leaders is the destruction of the socialist system and KOR, he wrote, would do this in three stages: firstly, by transforming Solidarity into a stronghold for KOR; secondly, by installing the kind of regime that existed in Poland prior to 1939, after having weakened the Polish Communist Party; finally, "if necessary, by getting rid of Lech Walesa, who is under the influence of Cardinal Wyszynski, and who has a centrist point of view."

Mr Kouznetsov could not be more wrong. A few days before his article appeared there was a meeting of KOR activists in which they seriously discussed formally dissolving KOR. Far from advocating the return to pre-war Poland, KOR has argued its position within a framework of socialist democracy, and it has rejected the nationalist revanchism of some of the political groupings and intellectuals that hover around Solidarity. Far from getting rid of Walesa, Kuron has seen himself become more marginalised since August 1980 to the extent that, by mid-summer 1981, it would be difficult to argue that he had any effective influence with the majority of the national leadership of Solidarity.

He was popular with the rank and file. I watched him intervene at a National Co-ordinating Commission meeting, and his comments were most attentively listened to by regional delegates. At a particularly tense time for Solidarity in November 1980, when the giant Warsaw steel plant, Huta Warsawa, threatened an all-out strike following the arrest of two Solidarity members, it was Kuron as much as Walesa, who persuaded them to go back to work. In May 1981 it was thanks to him and another KOR activist, Adam Michnik, that an extremely angry crowd on the point of riot over police treatment of two youngsters arrested in South Warsaw, was calmed down.

In an article in the 12th May 1981 issue of *Pravda,* KOR was accused of instigating Solidarity to brandish the weapon of a strike over unrealistic claims. The opposite is the truth. But what is KOR? Why does the Kremlin loathe it so much? What is its role in Solidarity?

KOR stands for Komitet Obrony Robotnikow — Workers' Defence Committee. In an open letter to the workers of the Baltic Coast, published after his release from prison on 1st September 1980 — one of the conditions of the final settlement of the Gdansk strike — Kuron described how and why KOR came into creation. "On 23rd September 1976, with over a dozen people, we formed the Workers' Defence Committee. We were ashamed that the intelligentsia had been silent in 1970 and '71, and we wanted to restore its good name. After the brutal suppression of workers' strikes and demonstrations, thousands of workers all over Poland

found themselves without jobs. Police stations were full. Trials
began in Warsaw (Ursus) and Radom. Thousands of workers were
brutally beaten and tortured. KOR set itself the aim of organising
financial help for people dismissed from work and the families of
the imprisoned; of offering legal and — when necessary — medical
help; of fighting for freedom for the imprisoned and jobs for the
sacked. The Workers' Defence Committee appealed to all Poles,
here and abroad, for moral and financial support and therefore
from the very start received large sums of money, since people both
at home and abroad responded generously to the appeal''. The
North American United Autoworkers' Union provided $10,000
(£5000) in response to this financial appeal from KOR.

The fact that the victims of the 1976 repression lived in or close
to Warsaw made the building of contacts between liberal and left-
wing intellectuals, many of them based in the capital, and workers,
that much easier. From the beginning KOR rejected clandestine activity. KOR members sent in their names and addresses to the
authorities and made no effort to hide what they were doing. To
begin with the work was not explicitly political or trade union
orientated. Rather, it concentrated on financial help to workers victimised after the 1976 repression. KOR members provided legal services and encouraged workers to begin court processes over
dismissals and loss of rights.

Workers were not told what to do, or even what direction to
think. Instead they were asked by intellectuals, "Look, how can we
help you? What do you need?" Observers attended trials. Sym-
pathetic lawyers revealed details of police brutality. In 1977 the
Workers' Defence Committee became the Committee for Social
Self-Defence (KSS), but continued to be known as KOR. At its
height the formal membership of the Committee was never more
than thirty-five. KOR sympathisers number many thousands, but
as a body it never developed a formal policy. There were no KOR
Congresses, no President or elected leadership. Although Kuron
became well-known through articles published in the West, and
thanks to his long history of persecution by the police, KOR was
not led or directed by him.

Robotnik

Throughout Labour Movement history, workers' papers have been
a key organising tool for the working class. The KOR activists
realised this straightaway. The most important thing they did was
to publish — to begin with, poorly stencilled, badly duplicated
news sheets. The writing concentrated on the problems of workers
and their families. The most important was *Robotnik* (The
Worker), which circulated in factories. Although its print run was

never more than 20,000, it was copied and passed from hand to hand.

It would be difficult to overestimate the importance of *Robotnik*. After the immediate need for financial and legal help for the victims of the 1976 repression had died away, the collection of material for, and preparation and distribution of, *Robotnik* maintained the link between socialist intellectuals and workers. In 1970, when striking workers marched past the Gdansk Polytechnic, the students refused to join the protest. They remembered 1968, when the workers failed to protest against the Moczar repression, and in some cases had even attacked students. It was to be one of KOR's main achievements after 1976 to repair this breach. Now young graduates and students play a useful role in the secretariat of Solidarity regions. Much more importantly, for the first time Polish workers had an organic link. Militants in one region or plant no longer felt completely isolated. They found their thoughts were shared by others. In *Robotnik* they found ideas put forward and arguments developed that they could use as a basis for discussion.

The authorities harassed KOR organisers, and arrested the senior KOR members now and then. But Gierek could not afford too severe a public crackdown. The Polish economy was becoming increasingly dependent on the West for financial credits and sale of advanced technology. The election of Jimmy Carter in 1976 saw a President in the White House who wanted to tie his foreign policy, in part, to the protection of human rights. In 1977 Carter visited Warsaw and publicly praised Poland's respect for human rights and religious freedom.

Gierek may also have thought that the 1976 workers' protests and the development of KOR reflected an economic discontent that would be solved by what he hoped, mistakenly, would be a more successful economic management of the country. In fact, the crisis was profoundly political. Unlike the radicals who raised their heads during the 1950's, but did so within a framework of reforming the Party and making the party-controlled institutions more democratic and accountable, the new generation of oppositionists wanted to see the role of the Party kept within limits, while other representative groups within Poland, (the peasants, the universities, the media, the lawyers, cultural workers and, most importantly, the trade unions), became independent of Party control and developed an autonomous role within the State.

In October 1980, by then several weeks after Gierek's downfall, the Polish State Prosecutor's office made this completely accurate summary of the development of the political opposition in the late 1970's: "The years 1977-80 saw the further organisational strengthening of contestatory elements. Besides KOR, other

organisations came into being, such as: The Movement for the
Defence of Human and Civil Rights; Students' Solidarity Committees; Peasants' Self-Defence Committees; The Movement of Young
Poland and The Confederation for Independent Poland. These
organisations gained ever wider influence by means, amongst
others, of large scale publishing and propaganda activities. About
30 periodical publications (newspapers, bulletins, magazines) were
being edited, printed and distributed. A number of new pamphlets
were published and several books printed. A number of titles appeared in several thousands of copies. Tens of thousands of leaflets
were distributed, spreading the views and slogans of anti-socialist
groups directed against established authority".

"Free" Trade Unions

If one ignores the phrase "anti-socialist", that summary could not
have been better made by KOR itself. But it is a mistake to lump
together all the opposition movements in the late 1970's. Some, like
the Confederation for an Independent Poland, led by a journalist,
Leszek Moczulski or the Movement of Young Poland, explicitly
looked to the dismantling of Poland's socialist State. It would also
be a mistake to assume that KOR represented the only opposition
in Poland after 1976. In the Ursus tractor factory a young worker,
only in his twenties, Zbigniew Bujak, organised discussion classes
with his fellow workers. Bujak was to emerge as leader of
Warsaw's region of Solidarity after September 1980. In February
1978, a "Workers' Committee" (later known as the Free Trade
Union of Silesia) was formed in Katowice. It called on Polish
workers to form "free national trade unions". The appeal, signed
by Kaimierz Switon and three other workers, attacked the "cen-
tralisation and omnipotence of the government machine, the lack
of independence of the official unions, and their consequent inability to defend workers' rights". "The Polish worker", they continued, "is alone and powerless. Only by uniting will we be able to
resist the exploitation of the workers by the State and the Party apparatus."

Katowice is in the heartland of mining and industrial Poland.
Switon himself ran a small electrical repair shop and had previously
brushed with the authorities by staging a hunger strike against a
plan to build a motorway across the pilgrims' route to Poland's
most important religious shrine at Czestochowa. He distributed
leaflets, which he produced locally, and acted quite independently
of KOR and other "free trade union groups". By 1979 he was
organising meetings of the free trade union group every Thursday
evening in a Katowice apartment.

In 1977, a free union "cell" was launched in Radom connected with *Robotnik;* while in May 1978, the Committee of the Free Trade Unions for the Baltic Coast was launched with a declaration by Andrzej Gwiazda, Antoni Sokolowski and Krzysztof Wyszkowski. It stated that the official unions had failed to protect the workers' interests and had turned into "a subordinate instrument for the organised exploitation of all social groups by the ruling Communist Party".

In October 1979 a Founding Committee of the Free Trade Unions of Western Pomerania was announced in Szczecin. In their founding statement they were explicit about the problems faced by workers, "such as the reform of the work norm to the detriment of the employees; wage losses caused by work interruptions that cannot be blamed on the workers; the unjust divisions of premiums and awards; the extension of working hours; inadequate conditions of hygiene and safety". Once again the workers concluded, "there is a need for the defence of workers' interests because the existing unions are unable to undertake such a defence".

The Szczecin committee drew inspiration from the Charter of Workers' Rights which was drawn up on the initiative of *Robotnik* and published in September 1979. Many of the demands that were to figure in the twenty-one demands put forward by the Gdansk strikers, and later to become the basic agreement between Solidarity and the government, are to be found in the 1979 Charter of Workers' Rights. These included wage increases, free Saturdays, improved safety protection, promotion based on merit rather than Party allegiance, an end to special shops for police and Party functionaries. (See Appendix for the full text of the Charter of Workers' Rights and the full text of the Gdansk Agreement). The Charter also gave due warning to the government by adding: "For several months now we have felt the effects of the crisis on our own skin. Deliveries and transport get worse and worse, wages are going down; in big plants the working hours are getting longer and taking up the 'free Saturday', there are more and more stoppages. If we ourselves do not now make a start at defending our own interests, our situation will go from bad to worse". The Charter was signed by representatives from twenty cities and towns in Poland.

The activists were also busy. In Silesia the Switon group distributed a leaflet protesting against the appalling safety conditions in the mines. Nearly sixty miners were killed in three separate explosions in Silesian mines in October 1979. Coal was one of Poland's biggest export earners and the pressure was constantly on to increase production at any price. In 1978 the hated four brigade system was introduced in order to bring in twenty-four hours a day production of coal. This rotating shift system involved six days work at irregular times of the day and night every week. Rest periods rarely coincided with moments when either family or friends were free.

The Silesian Free Trade Union Group reacted angrily to the introduction of the four brigade system. In a leaflet circulated in the pits, miners were told: "This system leaves no time to carry out the necessary repairs to secure your safety; it deprives you of free Sundays and disorganises leisure and family and religious life. You, mothers and wives of the miners, know it best. You, miners, understand well that our system has nothing to do with socialism; it is State capitalism in which there is not room for concern for workers' well-being. Miners are not important; the only thing that counts is the coal that can be exchanged for dollars. The Red bourgeoisie profit by your sweat, your injuries and often your lives. At the expense of working people they build themselves palaces equipped with modern gadgets imported from the West. It is they who build the luxury Party house at the cost of one thousand flats, for which you have to wait for years. The Party excuses itself with lack of resources, but does not stint money to develop the police forces which recruit healthy young men to spread fear and lawlessness in society, instead of employing them in useful work. There is no money, however, to spend on work safety."

Wage demands were also being put forward by workers in the Gdansk area. An attempt to introduce a new wage system without consultation in the Gdansk Northern Shipyards sparked off a two-day strike in October 1979. A joint Gdansk Free Trade Union — *Robotnik* leaflet circulated in November 1979, called for negotiations over the new wage structure. It is a sophisticated bargaining document, neither accepting nor rejecting the management proposals, but demanding that they conform to workers' needs. It is precisely the kind of information and group of demands that makes sense to a worker who is not likely to be over-interested in political questions. By early 1980, the groups of workers who helped distribute *Robotnik* in different towns, formed a more coherent body that was seeking to raise specific workers' issues, using language that made sense on the shopfloor.

The authorities became less tolerant of the increasing organisation of workers. In Cracow, a steelworker at the Lenin Steelworks, Mieczyslaw Gil, tried to raise workers' problems in articles he wrote for the official plant newspaper. He was threatened with dismissal for his pains. Switon was re-arrested and imprisoned. Edmund Zadrozynski, a former foundry worker in Grudziadz and *Robotnik* contributor, was sentenced to a prison term, after a trial that observers agreed was a farce.

1980

The growing repression reflected the worsening economic situation. Edward Gierek's massive gamble — to achieve, through soft loans and Western technology, a swift modernisation of Polish industry, which would simultaneously produce goods for export to earn hard currency, increase consumer goods production internally and either produce or import enough food to keep workers' stomachs full — had, by 1980, failed completely. The price Poland had to pay for Russian oil went up by the same amount — 130 per cent, the same as the price the West had to pay for Arab oil. The growing recession in the West, from the mid-1970's onwards, meant a declining export market for Polish goods. The much vaunted new technology imported from the West proved difficult to blend into existing Polish industry. The key function of new technology — to reduce labour costs — was almost irrelevant in a socialist State operating without a capitalist labour market. There was widespread bribery and corruption as government officials toured Western Europe and North America with budgets of millions of dollars to spend. At the same time, planning remained centralised and the planners continued to emphasise their beloved and easily controllable massive investments in heavy industrial plants, rather than the more complex small-scale manufacturing structures needed to produce goods that might still sell in a shrinking world market.

Once again, the rising expectations of the Polish population were disappointed by the badly managed economy. To reform the economy was a political task that would pose serious questions about the continuing influence and affluence of the Party cadres and managers that constituted Gierek's power base.

As ever, there was the question of food. The problem of food production in Poland has never been resolved. Three-quarters of the land is still in the hands of the peasants — there are three million separate farms or plots of land. The State has tried to collectivise some farms or persuade peasants to lease, sell or leave their farms to the State by means of inducements, such as offering State pensions to those willing to surrender land, or by making great difficulties in obtaining tractors or fertilisers for unco-operative peasants. The peasants' response has been to cut down production to what can be sold on peasant markets and what is needed for personal family subsistence. All efforts by the State to change the farming system have been viewed with great suspicion. Much as they are owners of tiny plots of land, peasants felt themselves to be at the mercy of the State's shifting policies. Peasants saw themselves as, in effect, disguised State labourers; which is why they set up, in 1981, what they insisted on calling a trade union — Rural Solidarity — rather than an association of small farmers.

Food dominates life in Poland as in no other European country. Shoppers spend an average of ninety minutes a day queuing. There is even a differential system of queues — one for ordinary shoppers, one for pregnant women and cripples. Fights have been known to break out because of complaints that someone was not sufficiently crippled to be entitled to wait in the faster moving cripples' queue. Shortages are endemic. If meat, for example, is available, sausage is not. A common sight is to see someone walking proudly home with, say, forty toilet rolls around his neck. If you go shopping in Poland, you buy as much as you can of any commodity you need, because you are never sure when you will see it again. Every Polish man and woman carries a little string bag in case they pass a shop in which food is available without having to queue. A large portion of the family budget went on buying food on the peasant market where prices were much higher, but at least food was available — that is, when the peasants were in a mood to produce it.

The inefficiency of Polish farming and the government's inability to come to terms with it was very expensive. In 1977 it was estimated that for every 100 zlotys spent by the consumer on food, the State was supporting the price with 70 zlotys. As the Polish economy worsened, the one way to redress the economy was to increase food prices. For the workers, it was the same as a State imposed wage cut.

The 30 per cent rise in meat prices was announced for 1st July 1980. (What the Government did was to transfer much of the better quality meat to shops that charged higher prices and that were normally patronised by Party and State officials. The effect — a price rise — was the same). In the West it was seen as a gesture to banks to whom Poland now owed US $20 billion. It showed that Gierek was ready to tighten the workers' belts in order to pay off interest owed to the West. A series of strikes hit different parts of Poland. In Lublin, in Eastern Poland, which is an important rail link with the Soviet Union, there was a region-wide strike that lasted three days between 16th July and 19th July 1980. Strikes were reported from all over Poland. After some hesitation, and faced with widespread strikes, the authorities became ready to negotiate with the strikers and ready, in many cases, to award wage increases that covered the meat price increases.

KOR activists and *Robotnik* contributors, often the same people, busied themselves producing special strike issues. They briefed Western journalists in Warsaw on what was taking place. For many Polish workers, and certainly for all the Party leadership, the only completely accurate source of information was Radio Free Europe, which, within hours of strikes taking place, was broadcasting details back to Poland.

The settlement of the Lublin strike seemed, at the time, to have cooled things down. Not every strike won a wage increase. Sometimes the promise of more meat being available in the shops was enough to persuade workers to return to their work. The repression of 1970 and 1976 was avoided. The government chose to negotiate. Workers, however, saw that by stopping work, they won immediate benefits. They asked themselves whether it would be possible to go beyond wage increases. When the workers of Gdansk showed they could, the ground was already well prepared to turn a strike in a Baltic shipyard into a national workers' movement that would, in due course, create a trade union representing 8-10 million workers.

Chapter 5

From Gdansk to Bydgoszcz

The signing of the Gdansk Agreement between the striking workers and the Polish government was shown on television screens all over the world. Lech Walesa, with his crucifix around his neck and a huge children's ballpoint pen topped with the Pope's portrait was in sharp contrast to the neatly dressed Polish Vice-Premier Miecyzslaw Jagielski. The government had already been reshuffled with several leading ministers and Prime Minister Babiauch losing their positions. On September 5th it was announced that the Polish Communist Party leader, Edward Gierek, had suffered a stroke and was stepping down. In short, the Polish workers had toppled their government. More important than that, they had secured new rights for themselves which could be used in defence of the gains made in August 1980 against future efforts to whittle them away. The signing of the Gdansk Agreement was to be followed by major crises over the registration of the new union, over its right to publish freely, and in March 1981, over the need for the physical safety of the union and its members to be guaranteed. Each one of these confrontations with the State showed Solidarity's hold over its membership and its ability to advance and maintain the position it had as a working-class organisation in Poland.

Talk to a miner in Silesia, a shipyard worker in Szczecin, or a steelworker in Katowice, and you will find that they are more than a little irritated with the concentration of attention on the strike in Gdansk. They too went on strike and signed agreements in August or early September 1980. For, if the strike had been limited to the Gdansk region in August 1980 it is doubtful that the government would have made the concessions it did. But as news of the Gdansk strike spread, workers in other parts of Poland joined in. The government at first cut off all telephone communications between Gdansk and the rest of Poland, but details of the twenty-one demands were smuggled out the of the Gdansk region (smuggled is perhaps too strong a word — road, rail and air links were never interrupted and all sorts of people could be pressed into taking leaflets and statements from the Lenin Shipyards to other parts of the country) and were reprinted by KOR activists and others. Foreign radio stations, such as Radio Free Europe and the BBC's Polish Service, broadcast details of the Gdansk strikes and the progress of the negotiations. The form of organisation set up in Gdansk, consisting of one representative of each striking factory or workplace who made up the Inter-Factory Strike Committee provided a simple model that workers in other cities could follow. By the second week of the Gdansk strike Poland was gripped in what was not far off a general strike. Miners in Silesia, transport workers in Wroclaw, steelworkers in Cracow and Warsaw, workers at the Ursus tractor factory in Warsaw, textile workers in Lodz, had also stopped work, formed Inter-Factory Strike Committees, occupied their workplaces and presented the same twenty-one demands as the Gdansk strikers. In Szczecin shipyard workers put forward a list of thirty-five demands. Workers elsewhere in Poland also followed closely another decision of the Gdansk Inter-Factory Strike Committee which ensured that the strike, although involving millions of workers and shutting down Poland's industrial production, as well as imports and exports vital for the Polish economy, did not touch essential public services such as water supplies, the central heating systems and tram and bus services. Health services were maintained and food distribution was relatively normal. There was no attempt to stop television and radio programmes or to call print workers out on strike. General strikes in the West often make their biggest impact because newspapers no longer appear, trains stop running and power supplies are threatened. Strikes that hit public services like hospitals, refuse collection or the post have proved deeply unpopular with the public, no matter the justness of the strikers' claims. The way the Gdansk Inter-Factory Strike Committee was formed with representatives of all sorts of different workplaces on it meant that workers in essential public services could be persuaded to continue providing them in exchange for a guarantee that their interests would be protected in negotiations with the government. And, as a reading of the Gdansk Agreement shows, the needs of the public services are prominent in the concessions made by the government. On the surface, then, life in Poland continued normally. People could go shopping, buy newspapers, watch television, not worry about water supplies or whether hospitals would be open. It was a signal to Moscow that the Polish general strike was not one that would follow traditional modes of protest in Eastern Europe. One of the first decisions of the Gdansk Inter-Factory Strike Committee was to ban the sale of vodka in the region during the strike. In all senses it was an intensely sober affair. The Polish government was trapped. It could not use the traditional arguments against previous workers' protests, i.e. that the country was threatened by chaos. There were no marches, no anti-Soviet slogans, no attacks on party buildings. Instead there was a widening general strike that was closing down Polish industry.

Even an appeal for moderation made by Cardinal Wyszynski in a televised broadcast on 26th August had failed to impress the strikers. The government representative in Gdansk, Vice-Premier Jagielski, was officially only talking to the Gdansk strikers. But he, and they, knew that the settlement would be for the whole of Poland. The entire Polish working class was pitched into the struggle and negotiations taking place in Gdansk.

As well as the working class, Poland's intelligentsia was also becoming heavily involved. It was Winston Churchill who said that 'intelligentsia' was a very nasty word for a very nasty thing, but in Poland the phrase intelligentsia or 'intellectuals' embraced a much broader section of society, stretching well beyond the ivory tower academic associations of the words in English. The Polish intelligentsia included teachers, lawyers, other members of the liberal professions, writers, film-makers, journalists, economists and sociologists. In the 1970's the Club of the Catholic Intelligentsia in Warsaw and in Cracow had provided a meeting place for those who wished to discuss ideas opposed to the ruling Communist Party. Academics organised seminars for university students all over Poland in private homes. This Association of Academic Courses popularly known as the "flying university", discussed forbidden subjects such as the role of the Polish Home Army during the war; Polish and Russian literature banned from official courses; or non-Marxist economics, and indeed, Marxist economics, though not the Polish State's variety. On 21st August 1980 an appeal, signed by sixty-four prominent intellectuals, was circulated in Warsaw. It expressed support for the striking workers "who are fighting for their, and our, right to a better life". Two of the appeal's organisers, Tadeusz Mazowiecki, editor of the liberal Catholic weekly *Wiez* (Link), and Professor Bronislaw Geremek, a world-famous medieval historian at Warsaw University, drove to Gdansk where they presented the appeal to Walesa. He asked them to stay on and help with negotiations. "We know what we want", he said, "but you are better at putting it into words". The two intellectuals called up their friends in Warsaw and the authorities reserved seats on the next morning's flight to Gdansk. By the beginning of the second week of the strike, the workers had their own commission of experts, ranging from the Catholic journalist Mazowiecki to the left-wing economist Tadeusz Kowalik. As with the Inter-Factory Strike Committees, the Gdansk model of having intellectuals as expert advisers was followed elsewhere in Poland. It drew on the energy of local university teachers and lawyers who could draft statements, and express in an ordered manner, the needs of the workers. The intellectuals were not asked to submerge their identity in a kind of phoney 'workerism'; nor, on the other hand, could they in any way manipulate the workers. The open democratic style of decision-making inside the Inter-Factory Strike Committees meant that intellectuals could put forward proposals, but it was the workers who would vote and decide upon them.

By the end of August the Polish government had run out of cards to play. A hidden general strike was crippling the country; there were no street disturbances to justify physical repression; the Church had failed to cool down the strikers; the Polish intelligentsia had joined forces with the working class; the government had to make all the concessions — restoring telephone communications, promising full payment for days on strike, while intense international media interest narrowed other possible options for action. It all added up to that sinking feeling that every negotiator, whether representing employer or workers, sooner or later has to face when he or she is in a position that is getting weaker day by day, or even hour by hour. The time comes when you simply have to give in and hope that in another fight on another day you will win back what your weakness forced you to concede. Thus it was with the Polish government who even wearily conceded the release of KOR activists in order to stop the strike, get things back to work, and restore normality. There is no doubt that that is what Jagielski thought he was doing as he signed the agreement in Gdansk on 31st August 1980. But a return to pre-August 1980 relationships between workers and local managers, regional officials, Party leaders and the government, was not possible. Another government minister had signed a separate agreement with the Inter-Factory Strike Committee in Szczecin, and negotiations were continuing with steelworkers and miners in Silesia. At that stage the government thought it had signed a local agreement with the Gdansk strikers. Although provisions in it were clearly of national application, such as the right to form independent trade unions, there was no agreed machinery set up to make the Gdansk Agreement effective on a nationwide basis.

The Spirit of Gdansk Spreads

As part of the Gdansk Agreement, its twenty-one points were published in the official press so the whole country could see what the strikers had won. Everywhere workers turned to local managers and regional authorities and, in effect, said, "We'll have the same as Gdansk, please". The promise of a 2000 zlotys wage increase was left to negotiations on an industry-by-industry basis. This irritated workers, who saw it as a disguised way of re-introducing industrial trade unionism and re-asserting the role of the discredited official trade unions, which were organised by industry. In different regions and different industries, managers and government representatives handled workers' demands differently. The effect of all this, in regions where the authorities were obstructive, was to produce a wave of rolling, spontaneous strikes all over Poland in the first weeks of September 1980. Strikes took place in Bialystok, Bydgoszcz, Mielec, Opole and Zakopane; and in many other areas of Poland.

Everywhere workers elected their own plant committees and came together to form Inter-Factory Committees in the cities and big towns. If the Polish government hoped that the Gdansk Agreement would be limited only to the Baltic coast, or that its provisions could be watered down elsewhere in Poland, their calculations were wrong. Instead, many workplaces that had left the actual business of striking to the big, powerful plants during August 1980, now went on strike themselves and organised a democratic internal union structure. Eighteen thousand workers at an aeroplane factory in Mielnik went on strike in protest against being asked to sign a petition denouncing the new union. Regional Inter-Factory Committees were demanding to see the Voivod (Regional Prefect) and obliging him, under pressure, or just the threat of a strike, to concede the Gdansk points locally. Hundreds of thousands of workers who had been supportive onlookers up to 31st August, now went through the same process as the August strikers. Because of a refusal to make the Gdansk Agreement applicable to all Poland's workers, they had to organise, make links with local intellectuals, often go on strike and elect their own leaders. They found they could negotiate with factory managers and Voivods, that they could produce their own bulletins, and, unsurprisingly, they developed a taste for workers' power. As Zbigniew Przydzial, a boatyard worker from Wroclaw, put it: "Unions are only any good if they are born in struggle". It would be wrong to suppose that everywhere the workers met with opposition. Many factory managers or regional officials welcomed the new movement as a force that could curb corruption and force decision makers at the top to make decisions based on wider and more realistic factors. An old Polish joke is set in the interview room, where a would-be Party official is being interviewed by the selection committee: "Please explain to us, comrade", asked the committee, "what is the difference between capitalism and socialism?" "In capitalism there is tyranny, inequality, injustice, misery, hatred between nations, war, oppression, corruption, class struggle: in socialism we have freedom, good life, equality, brotherhood of nations, progress, justice, peace." "Very good, comrade. The next question: What is today the most important task of our Party and of the country?" "To catch up and surpass capitalism!" Undoubtedly part of the reason for the successful growth of post-war Western capitalism (at least through the 1950's and 1960's) was the existence of strong trade unions that put firms under constant pressure to produce as efficiently as possible under the pressure of constantly rising labour costs.

The lack of independent trade unions in Communist States has meant the absence of an important independent social force that, in capitalist countries, helps shape economic, as well as political, decisions. For those in power at all levels in Poland who wanted to see the country's economic and social relations rescued from the effects of the disastrous decisions of the Gierek era, the existence of the new union, Solidarity, was not necessarily unwelcome, provided, of course, it stuck firmly to a trade union role. In regions around Wroclaw, Gdansk and Szczecin, the new union and the authorities settled down to a reasonable relationship. In other areas, such as Radom and Czestochowa, the regional voivodships put as many difficulties as possible in the way of Solidarity. In the six months after the signing of the Gdansk Agreement there was a report almost every two weeks of this or that government, regional or party official being made to resign after protests, strikes or sit-ins by Solidarity members. Not all of these changes can, or should be, attributed directly to the new union. The changes that followed Gierek's downfall would be reflected all the way down Poland's governing and political hierarchy. Inefficient, lazy or unpopular office holders would become much more vulnerable as the ruling apparatus lost all stability and cohesiveness. Different factions within the government or Communist Party would use the existence of Solidarity and the need, either to come to terms with it, or to try and curb its activities as a justification for the policies or personnel changes they were advocating.

For Solidarity, the six months that followed the signing of the Gdansk Agreement seemed to be a long struggle to maintain its existence as an independent trade union. Three major moments of crisis stand out in the middle of a long list of incidents that saw the new union and the authorities square up to each other. From each crisis Solidarity learnt more about itself and about its role and position in Poland.

Registration

The first major test came over the registration of the new union. On 24th September 1980, Solidarity deposited its statutes for legal approval before a court in Warsaw. Originally drawn up for the Gdansk Inter-Factory Committee, the statutes were accepted as covering the whole of the country when representatives from more than 30 regions met in Gdansk in mid-September 1980, and decided to form a national Solidarity organisation. The statutes were drawn up by the Commission of Experts that was now working full time for Solidarity. In a pamphlet published in English for foreign visitors, Solidarity described the statutes this way: "The statutes lay down the fundamental principle of the Union's activities. The Union, being independent, declares itself to be non-political. This means that it has no intention of performing functions of a political party, nor is it desirous of governing the State. It abides by the fundamental lines of politics of the Polish authorities, thus accepting the leading role of the Party in affairs of State. This means also, that it is open to all, irrespective of their political opinions, their religious beliefs and the organisations to which they belong". The pamphlet is not an inaccurate description of Solidarity's statutes and public political position as it was in the middle of 1981, but at the time of the formal legal registration of the new union, the question of whether the leading role of the Communist Party should be included in the actual statutes came close to provoking a general strike and gave rise to the biggest stand-off between union and government since the August strikes. The new statutes were deposited with a Warsaw court on 24th September 1980 in order that the union might be formally registered. By the middle of October there was no word from the court. Solidarity was busy organising itself, getting offices, putting out bulletins, enrolling members, and sometimes running strikes. But it was doing all of these things in a legal vacuum. Although it had successfully organised a one-hour strike on 3rd October 1980, in protest at official slowness in implementing the Gdansk Agreement, officially it had no legally recognised national presence.

There was the added irritation that the old industrial unions were busy changing their names so as to include the description "independent self-governing" in their title. This fooled no-one in Poland, but outside the country it enabled the government to talk about a general trade union renewal process in which Solidarity was just one among many new independent unions that were springing up all over Poland. Western commentators used to refer to Solidarity as the largest of Poland's new unions, until reporters finally realised that the other "independent self-governing" unions were simply the old Party-controlled unions under a change of title.

On 24th October 1980 the Warsaw court handed down its ruling on Solidarity's statutes. The court was willing to accept them, but had added a clause which specifically recognised the leading role of the Polish United Workers' Party — Poland's Communist Party. The union exploded with anger. The court had arbitrarily added a clause about the leading role of the Party without any consultation with Solidarity. It was not that the new union rejected the party's leading role (though one Solidarity member told me that Polish workers wanted the party to have a leading role in the same way that the King of the Belgians had a leading role in his country!) but they refused to have their statutes, which defined in writing what the new union would be, altered by a judge, in a way that legally implied Solidarity's tutelage to the party. As Solidarity pointed out, Clause I of the Gdansk Agreement stated that the union "will recognise the leading role of the PUWP in the State, and will not oppose the existing system of international alliances". It was one thing to have that in an agreement negotiated between two sides. It was another for a union that had thought hard about how it perceived itself and had decided that it would avoid any formal self-description that identified it publicly in a party political sense, now to be told by a middle-ranking judge, clearly acting on orders from above, that he was going to re-write the statutes. The anger over the Warsaw court judgement reflected the pent-up frustration inside Solidarity over the slowness of so many regional authorities in implementing the letter, let alone the spirit, of the Gdansk Agreement. The strike wave of September did not die away, and sporadic strikes kept bursting out in October. On 28th October 1980, the National Co-ordinating Commission met in Gdansk and announced a general strike for 12th November unless Poland's Supreme Court had agreed to remove the offending new clause from the union's statutes. Leaflets were prepared by regional Solidarity committees, instructing workers to occupy plants, to bring food and bedding with them, banning alcohol, and other preparations for the strike. There was a short warning strike which was obeyed throughout Poland. In Warsaw, tram drivers left their trams stationary in the middle of the city. Poland's leaders were left in no doubt that Solidarity meant business.

The Polish government and the Warsaw Pact countries also increased the pressure. Kania flew to Moscow, while East Germany and Czechoslovakia closed their borders with Poland. Western journalists were kept out of Poland and Polish television showed film of Soviet troop manoeuvres. The pressure had no effect and there was no sign of the workers' nerves breaking. On the 10th November 1980, the Supreme Court reversed the lower court's ruling, and struck out the offending reference to the leading role of the Party.

The discussion over the importance of the clause is almost irrelevant. What had happened was, that the Polish State had selected that terrain to try and claw back some of the advances made by Solidarity, and had been decisively rebuffed.

Arresting Solidarity Printers

The victory over the statutes was closely followed by a second ma-

jor crisis when the police arrested Solidarity's chief printer in Warsaw, Jan Narozniak. They did so because Solidarity in Warsaw had
printed and distributed a copy of a memorandum prepared in the
Chief Prosecutor's office describing Solidarity as "anti-socialist",
and outlining legal ways in which the authorities might move
against the new union. The police also arrested Piotr Sapielo, a
junior clerk in the Chief Prosecutor's office, who was accused of
leaking the document. Steelworkers at Huta Warszawa and
workers at the Ursus tractor factory, went on strike, demanding the
release of the two men. The strike was officially supported by the
Warsaw region of Solidarity. Leaflets were printed saying: "Today, Narozniak. Tomorrow, Walesa. The day after, you." The
Warsaw leadership of Solidarity went further and drew up a list of
five demands, calling for an investigation into the activities of the
militia, the secret police and the Ministry of the Interior, and a
reduction in the budgets of the security police and militia. They
also wanted those responsible for the repression of 1976 brought to
justice.

The government released the two Solidarity activists and promised further talks on the five demands. Lech Walesa and Jacek
Kuron had to go in person to the steelworkers. The Solidarity
leadership was in a quandary. Having obtained the release of the
two men, it now had a strike by two important Polish factories over
the politically extremely sensitive question of the security forces.
Although the five demands had been approved by the Warsaw
region, the strike over these demands had not been sanctioned by
the Gdansk-based national leadership. One of Solidarity's senior
advisers told me that the strike reflected the slightly uneasy relationship existing between Gdansk and Warsaw. The Warsaw
workers wanted to make their own history by securing a major
diminution of the powers of the security forces, and to show that
they too could achieve changes in Polish society similar to those
secured by Gdansk workers in the August agreement.

Yet to confront so unambiguously the power of the security
forces was very risky. To ask that their budgets be reduced was to
alarm the Polish army, which could expect that its generous
budgetary allocation would be next on the list, if the security
forces' finances were trimmed. With the release of the two men,
Solidarity had won a handsome victory. The strike told the government that having legally recognised the new union, the workers
would expect the government to abide by the spirit of that recognition, and then would act decisively to ensure that the union would
protect its members and their workers' right to publish what was
considered important to read.

Lech Walesa and Jacek Kuron went to Huta Warszawa to explain to the striking workers that their demands on the security forces would have to be shelved. The workers were confused and angry. After all, the five demands had been drafted by the Warsaw regional leadership and now they were being told that their strike to secure the demands was no longer opportune. They went back to work, but the grumbles about the lack of 100 per cent certainty of purpose amongst the Solidarity leadership were to continue for weeks afterwards.

In November 1980 Solidarity ordered an end to pay demands and strikes. Partly it was worried about the inflationary pressure of wage increases won by strikes, but workers were also getting tired. As Maciek Stolwiski, a 30-year-old turner at the Ursus tractor factory, told me in December 1980: "We have been on strike five times in five months: in July over food prices, in August over Gdansk, in October over pay, and twice in November over the registration of Solidarity and the arrest of Narozniak and Sapielo. Now we are tired of strikes. I think if we were asked to strike again we wouldn't, unless it were of exceptional importance".

At the beginning of the New Year the government tried to weaken Solidarity through insisting, contrary to the Gdansk Agreement that Saturdays would still be considered as working days. The government plan was to present Solidarity as economically irresponsible and to try and atomise different sections of Solidarity by offering bonuses and other benefits to certain selected groups of workers for Saturday working. The economic argument had some force, though some Katowice steelworkers told me that working Saturdays would not automatically resolve the economic problems: "We worked six days and more before, and the economy was still disastrous. The answer is to be found in better management and equipment, not in working the Polish worker to death". In a statement Solidarity declared its willingness to negotiate the problem of a 5-day week, but said that without accurate economic statistics it could not judge the honesty of the government's claim that Saturday working was necessary to improve the Polish economy. "Many working hours per week are lost as workers wait for raw materials or semi-finished products. Cuts in electricity supply alone make everybody idle. Improvements here would probably be more important in terms of production than losses caused by shorter working hours". The National Co-ordinating Commission also tartly declared that it had noted a less flexible attitude by the government since the union had called for a halt to pay increase demands and strikes at the end of November. Solidarity told its members to take off the Saturday in January the government had announced as a working day. It was not quite a strike, but it was a way of withdrawing labour to make a point. An uneasy compromise was reached at the end of January, whereby the government agreed to three free Saturdays out of four. But, once again, it was an indication that the Gdansk Agreement was not to be fully honoured, and even when its provisions were partially implemented, it needed a strike to get the government to stand by its side of the agreement.

Gradually Solidarity was realising that its most effective weapon — an all-out national strike — was rather like the nuclear bomb. It could be used, but how many times? It could be threatened, but what happened if the government failed to back down under the threat? For the rest of the winter Lech Walesa and the other Solidarity leaders travelled around Poland trying to calm down strikes. But Walesa was conscious of criticisms that he was becoming too cautious. At Bielsko-Biala, in southern Poland, where workers went on strike, demanding the dismissal of local officials, Walesa rejected government threats and told workers to stand by in case there was an attack on Bielsko-Biala: "If that happens and communications are broken off, organise occupations and prepare for passive resistance". In many smaller regions lacking the workers' experience of having won major victories in August or September 1980, the Party and regional authorities were still behaving arrogantly towards Solidarity. There were many reports of physical attacks on Solidarity leaders and the spreading of anti-Solidarity propaganda.

The Militia Attacks in Bydgoszcz

The tension building up all winter in Poland was finally released by the Bydgoszcz incident in March 1981. All through the winter Poland's peasants, who had organised themselves into Rural Solidarity, had been pressing the government for recognition and similar negotiating rights to industrial Solidarity. The same Warsaw court that had tried to alter Solidarity's statutes had refused them legal recognition, arguing that as individual self-employed workers, they could not have trade union status. Peasants had occupied the premises of the official unions in Rezeszow in January. On 17th March 1981, in Bydgoszcz, they launched an occupation of the offices of the United Peasant's Party — a communist controlled Party that was meant to represent peasants' interests. In their view it was the only way they could force their claim for an independent organisation to the attention of the authorities. Solidarity in Bydgoszcz, a large industrial and chemical centre of 400,000 workers, about 150 miles west of Warsaw, decided to back the peasants and called for a demonstration outside the meeting of regional council on 19th March 1981, at which Solidarity leaders, who had been invited to the meeting, promised to raise the peasants' demands. The chairman of the regional council, using the old bureaucrats' trick, adjourned the meeting without reaching the item on the agenda covering the peasants. In protest, the Solidarity leaders refused to leave the meeting room, and after a seven-hour wait, in which they were joined by regional councillors, they were dragged out by local militia men who had arrived in force. Three of them, including Jan Rulewski, the chairman of Bydgoszcz Regional Solidarity, were beaten up so badly by the militia they had to stay in hospital.

Despite government propaganda that the incident was somehow Solidarity's fault and that outside provocateurs had beaten up Rulewski, the details of the incident and the cold-blooded beating up of the Solidarity leaders spread all over Poland. Posters, leaflets and cassette tapes about the Bydgoszcz incident quickly appeared. The refusal to permit Rural Solidarity's legal registration was producing strains all over Poland, not dissimilar to the tension leading up to Solidarity's registration.

Although the new Prime Minister, General Jaruzelski, had called for a 90-day moratorium on strikes on taking up office in February, it would have been impossible for Solidarity to allow such a violent, physical attack against its senior representatives to take place without the strongest response. In addition, there had been several other unexplained attacks on Solidarity activists in different towns. At the National Co-ordinating Commission the anger was such that only a general strike was seen as an adequate response. But a general strike to secure what? The question was raised, but never properly answered.

The strike was called for 31st March and a four-hour strike, four days previously, was supported by all of Poland's workers. Once again Solidarity had shown that it could shut down the country and that its orders would be obeyed. The government started to back off, and on 28th March produced a long report which criticised the behaviour of the authorities and the militia in Bydgoszcz. In a sentence, which deserves to be included in any dictionary of civil service quotations, the report said; "It is the opinion of the commission that medical evidence concerning the extent of the injuries does not provide grounds to assert that these injuries were self-inflicted". The report was read out in full on Saturday night television and indicated that the government was not yet ready to confront a full-scale strike. The only way a general strike could be beaten was by military intervention, which would necessitate the use of Soviet troops. That awful realisation still hangs over both the Polish government and Solidarity, and it is difficult to say which is more hampered in its range of options by the threat. On 26th March the chairman of the Bydgoszcz regional council 'resigned'. In discussion with Solidarity representatives the government promised that it would move a legal registration of Rural Solidarity, but it rejected the demands for the immediate punishment of the militia officers and those who had given them their orders to beat up Rulewski and his colleagues.

The National Praesidium of Solidarity met on Monday 30th March to discuss the government offer. A dispute broke out between Lech Walesa and his deputy, Andrzej Gwiazda. All participants agreed that a general strike was now politically extremely dangerous, but a major row broke out over the nature of democracy and decision making inside the union. Gwiazda, strongly supported by Karol Modzelewski, said that as the National Co-ordinating Commission, consisting of representatives of all the Solidarity regions, had called the strike only the same body could call it off. The National Praesidium, or rather that section of it in Warsaw to negotiate with the government, could not usurp its powers. Walesa, supported by a majority of Praesidium members present, retorted that to delay a decision and call a meeting of the full National Co-ordinating Commission would suggest that the strike was definitely going ahead and might force the government to begin counter measures that would considerably worsen the already horribly tense situation.

It was a classic trade union problem in which workers' leaders have to take decisions which either betray the purest commitment to democratic consultation, or which expediently avoid a potentially disastrous situation developing, but may leave workers thinking that key decisions are being made behind their backs. Walesa's point of view won out and, although Karol Modzelewski resigned his position as National Solidarity Press Officer, in protest at the way the decision was taken, there can be no doubt that both Polish workers and Polish society were relieved that the general strike was called off.

According to Walesa, they had won 70 per cent of what they were after. It is unlikely that anyone will ever know at what level the attack by the militia was ordered, or to what extent the whole incident was premeditated by the authorities. In June 1981 Bydgoszcz policemen said that orders for handling the incident came from outside Bydgoszcz. Stefan Bratkowski, one of Poland's most respected journalists, and a senior Party member, wrote an open letter to the Party immediately after the Bydgoszcz incident, in which he accused unnamed senior Party officials of being "men who try to set the force of public order against their own community so as to have no way out except to fight it out". He added, "Our hardliners stand for no programme except of confrontation and misinformation. They promise us nothing but drama. Today they are trying to involve the whole Party leadership and the govern-

ment in a clash with the entire society. With incalculable consequences, they are trying to provoke society to behaviour justifying
the use of force."

The fact that the government and Party headed away from a confrontation, and that Solidarity accepted less than its full demands
helped to clear the tension that had been accumulating in Poland
during the long winter months of 1980-1. By May 1981 Rural
Solidarity was both legally registered and approved of by the Polish
government. Talking at the Bydgoszcz regional Solidarity headquarters six weeks after he had been beaten up, a fully recovered
Jan Rulewski said that much had changed since the Bydgoszcz incident: "Everyone is now turning to us for help. The local press is
more open and the local intellectuals are giving us more help. The
local militia now refuse to move unless they have a signed order in
writing".

But Rulewski went on to stress Solidarity's claims that were still
outstanding: freedom for political prisoners, an end to censorship,
economic reform, and respect for law. He went on: "We have two
ways out — either to strike all the time, or to try and make our life
more democratic so that we can solve our problems without using
the strike threat. We need to be more involved in decisions. But only if we have a real influence. We don't want to be mere decorations".

Nearly nine months after the signing of the Gdansk Agreement
Rulewski was echoing the opinions of the workers and intellectuals
who had helped to produce and negotiate the historic document
signed on 31 August 1980. An important point Solidarity constantly stresses is, that no new claims have been put forward. All the
disputes and conflicts have been over persuading the government to
honour both the letter and spirit of the Gdansk Agreement. Attempts to wriggle out of the Gdansk Agreement have not weakened
Solidarity. On the contrary, it would appear that from each crisis it
drew lessons and never let itself be provoked into a response which
could be used as an excuse for more drastic forms of intervention
and repression. After March 1981 one could see a curious bifurca-
tion policy carried out in Poland. After the Bydgoszcz incident, incidents involving militia or police harassment of Solidarity
members, distribution of anti-Solidarity propaganda, seizure of
Solidarity publications, and other examples of officially sanctioned
bullying continued to be reported. At the same time, Solidarity was
able to launch its own national journal, gain official access to the
media, move to bigger premises in Warsaw and Gdansk, see Rural
Solidarity registered, and survive the death of Cardinal Wyszynski,
without a major crisis.

An important sign of trade union development is the capacity not to turn every example of anti-union harassment into an occasion for a general strike. On the other hand, once basic principles of a trade union's rights to organise and carry on its activities are compromised, then trade unionism starts to lose ground. Despite all the obstacles placed in its way, no amount of official obscurantism or direct harassment seemed to stop Solidarity from organising and getting on with its job. In its first period of existence each crisis seemed to make the union stronger.

Chapter 6

The Structure and
Organisation of Solidarity

The way a trade union movement is structured in any given country reflects its origin, its policies, and sometimes the nature of the employers that it confronts. Thus, in Britain, the long tortuous growth of trade unionism over 150 years has meant a confusing mixture of craft, industrial and general unions — still more than 100 in total — with a national trade union centre, the Trades Union Congress, that has great influence, but little direct power. When the management of the British Steel Corporation sits down at the negotiating table, it faces seventeen different unions. In West Germany, by contrast, the steel employers have to deal with only one union, the 2.7 million-strong IG Metall, which organises all workers in the steel and metal industry. West German unions were reborn after 1945 with help and advice from the TUC. Both the West German trade unionists themselves and their British advisers were determined that they would have strong industrial unions, with all the workers in any industry belonging to the same union. There was to be no repetition of pre-war German unionism, under which workers found themselves split along craft, industrial, political, and even religious, lines.

Another form of trade union organisation is to be found in France, Italy and Spain, where a worker joins a union because of a shared political tendency. Thus, the union confederations — there are no fully autonomous industrial unions in the British, American, West German or Swedish sense — are closely connected with either a political party or a political point of view: Communist, Socialist or non-political (though confederations that claim the latter status are usually fanatically anti-Communist, and thus define their political position negatively). A very crude division in the different style of organisation of trade unions would be between Protestant and Catholic countries. In the former, trade unions developed as mutual aid workers' organisations. Their politics always took a second place to the job of defending workers' economic interests. In France, Italy, Spain, and to a certain extent in Germany, in the late 19th and early 20th century, trade unions were under the control of, or were seen as the industrial offshoots of, political parties. In 1891 a Papal encyclical, *Rerum Novarum* (New Things), acknowledged the workers' need for trade unions, but warned against the atheistic influence of Socialist ideology. The Catholic Church actively encouraged and helped finance the establishment of trade unions which rejected Marxist or Socialist politics. They became known as confessional unions and, although their successors have 'deconfessionalised' themselves, and, in general, moved closer to a social democratic position, there is still considerable division, and sometimes open political warfare, between the union confederations, reflecting different political tendencies in France, Spain, Italy, and especially in Latin America.

Another important aspect of trade union structure which marks off different national trade union systems, is the role and power of the national centre. In Britain the TUC, in the United States the AFL-CIO, and in West Germany the DGB do not negotiate with employers, nor do they have the power, for example, to command or to stop industrial action. Their role is to articulate general union needs and policy, and, in particular, to maintain relations with the government and to lobby the legislature to protect workers' and unions' interests, either by proposing laws or regulations that will strengthen or protect the unions, or by fighting against the passing of anti-union legislation. In Sweden, by contrast, the Swedish equivalent of the TUC, the LO, negotiates the framework of the annual wage agreement on behalf of all Sweden's blue collar workers.

Despite the many different models, and the very many imperfections of Western trade unions, they are linked by having a common formal commitment to democratic control by the membership. There are often arguments over the respective democratic worth of postal ballots, appointed or elected officials, congresses every single, or only every four years, or the power of the union bureaucracy to crush dissent but, in essence, the unions in the West are controlled by democratic means. The leaders of most European and American unions are most often workers who have worked their way up. Compare this with the Soviet Union where Alexander Shelepin moved easily from being head of the KGB to being head of the Russian trade union movement. From the very beginning of the Soviet Union's existence, trade unions were placed firmly under Party control. According to Lenin, the main role of unions in a Communist State was to increase production. The Soviet model of a supreme national trade union centre to which industrial unions were subordinated was installed in Eastern Europe after 1945. In Poland there was the Central Council for Trade Unions (CRZZ) and under it a metalworkers' union, railwaymen's union, a print workers' union, and so on. Although in some cases delegates to higher councils of the industrial (or branch, as they are known in Poland) unions could be genuinely elected from the base, notably in the years 1956-57, and in 1971, the top echelons of the unions were filled by Party nominations. The industrial unions never took up workers' cases and sided with management in disciplining or dismissing militants.

Organisation by Region, not Industry

The leaders of the workers who emerged victorious from the Gdansk strike with their Agreement, in which the government had conceded their right to form independent, self-governing unions, had many different, non-Polish, models to choose from. Before 1939, Polish trade unions were a disastrous mixture of Socialist, Communist, Catholic and Jewish unions split, in addition, on craft, industrial and regional lines, and always under tremendous pressure from the reactionary pre-war Polish governments. They provided no model for Solidarity to follow. The new workers' leaders knew what they did not want. They did not want to reproduce the trade union system which they had just decisively rejected. Both the opulent operating style and the industrial organisation of the old unions were, and are, spurned by Solidarity. Instead, the workers, their leaders and their expert advisers have had to develop a new form of union organisation which is unique to Poland.

The key to Solidarity's organisation is that it is based on a regional structure. Poland is divided into forty-nine administrative districts (voivodships) run by a centrally appointed regional administrator (the voivod). As the strike in the Lenin Shipyard developed, many other plants and factories in the Gdansk voivodship joined in.

They formed themselves into an Inter-Factory Strike Committee (MKS) and elected an executive committee or praesidium, with workers from different types of factories or professions. As news of the Gdansk strikes spread, different groups of workers in other regions also went on strike. They too formed a regional MKS and elected local leaders from more than one workplace. Thus, from the very beginning, Solidarity was organised on a geographical basis. Workers drew strength from the sense of unity and mutual solidarity provided by organising all workers within a town or region, irrespective of industry or profession.

Solidarity appears determined to stick by its original structure and very little sympathy is expressed for any kind of industrial structure, i.e. all the steel workers in one union, all the teachers or transport workers in their own separate unions. Partly, this is explained by the fact that the old unions were organised industrially and there is a hatred for anything that seems to resemble the old unions. There is an often-expressed commitment to strong unions helping the weak — miners or steelworkers threatening strike action unless health service workers had their demands met. The sharing egalitarianism of grouping widely differing categories of workers in the same regional structure was stressed by Andrzej Gwiazda almost as if it had a specific moral worth.

Solidarity is also putting forward demands relating to the community: the organisation of public transport, or food distribution, or problems connected with education or the environment, which have to be negotiated with the Voivod, who wields considerable regional administrative power. In fact, considerable economic, social and political power rests at the regional level, and as a consequence Solidarity is mirroring the actual power structure that exists in Poland. With the State owning all industry and being the sole employer, one of the key factors that justifies industrial unionism in the West (the need for unity of all workers in an industry in order to tackle separate employers in the same industry), does not exist in Poland. If anything, the support for the regional organisation of Solidarity has strengthened since the union's creation. Although there has been a modest inter-steel plant coordinating committee, it has not, so far, played a major role beyond a few meetings with the Minister for Heavy Industry. But the organisational preference for a regional, as opposed to an industrial, structure, is by no means a permanently settled affair. Talking to leaders of Solidarity in the Huta Warszawa steel plant near Warsaw in May 1981, I was told that the inter-steel plant committee had not played a major role, but it was important that it was kept in existence. One of them put it this way: "Steelworkers are only eleventh in the industrial wage league table. We need to put this right. Obviously there is a difficulty in co-ordinating our demands with the rest of Solidarity. We know that we need better contact with other workers in the steel industry, but at the moment the regional structure is more important. There could be no question, as far as I can see, of there being a steel industry strike. We will continue to work within the region".

The regional structure of Solidarity means that in each city or town there is one central focus to which all workers can turn for help, irrespective of what kind of work they do. If Solidarity had to divide and spread its available leadership and expert advice on an industrial as well as a regional basis, the quality of that leadership would be considerably diluted. With a regional structure it is less likely that one would see develop so easily that rivalry between blue collar and white collar unions, which is one of the hallmarks of Western trade unionism. The strength that Solidarity draws from its regional structure was implicitly acknowledged in a speech made in March 1981 by Andrzej Zabinski, the Party chief in Katowice, a Politburo member, and one of the anti-Solidarity hardliners in the

Party apparatus in Silesia. Zabinski was addressing a group of senior police and security service officers in Katowice about how to deal with Solidarity, and he told them: "First of all we have to mount a political attack on the principle of union regions, the principle proclaimed by Mr Walesa or those who prompt him. We have to attack this principle very strongly by asking them thousands of questions. What about the miners' property, for example? Are the miners to be together with the hairdressers? Where in the world do you have such trade unions? This is truly a soft spot for political attack. We have to attack, we simply have to attack now".

Inside Solidarity's Offices

Solidarity is housed in an immense variety of buildings. The national headquarters in Gdansk is a former seamen's hotel. In the Summer of 1981, Solidarity will move to a larger hotel opposite Gdansk railway station. In Warsaw, Solidarity moved in the Summer of 1981 from occupying a few floors in a residential block of a research institute, whose occupants protested bitterly at having to make way for the union. The premises have been made available by local administrations. They are usually in run-down buildings that lack all but the barest amenities. An exception is in Katowice, where Solidarity is housed in a large mock Gothic detached house which was used as a Gestapo headquarters during the war, and later became a kind of private club for top managers in the region. Well-carpeted rooms with comfortable sofas and armchairs, give the Katowice office of Solidarity a different atmosphere from other Solidarity premises.

Each Solidarity building is efficiently divided up into different rooms: the regional chairman's office, finance office, printing office, election committee's office, legal aid office, plus several interview rooms. In all of them there is a constant coming and going, and a busy, noisy atmosphere.

Although the major Solidarity regions are connected by telex (it is quite easy to make instant contact with Solidarity by telex from outside Poland) there is a shortage of telephones, and nearly all office equipment. Apart from gifts from the West, much of Solidarity's office equipment is either very old, or is begged, borrowed or liberated from offices in which the union's presence is strong.

Solidarity does not object to having to exist in shabby, run-down accommodation. Firstly, many Solidarity members associate large, well-decorated offices with the much disliked old unions. Secondly, in the words of Professor Bronislaw Geremek, one of Solidarity's leading advisers: "Poland is a poor country. Solidarity cannot be seen to be richer than the general level of life in Poland".

The problem of finding at least reasonably sized premises was one of the testing grounds between Solidarity and the authorities in the first months of the union's existence. In areas like Wroclaw or Gdansk there was no problem, thanks to good relations between Solidarity and the authorities. Elsewhere, regional and party authorities made as many difficulties as possible for Solidarity in its search for an office. There were several local strikes or occupations to apply the necessary pressure.

The kind of problem faced by Solidarity in its search for premises was revealed at a meeting I attended in December 1980 of the praesidium of Radom Solidarity. They had been given offices which were formerly those of the old unions, but had organised a sit-in and a short protest strike late in November in order to obtain their own premises. Now they had been offered new premises, but they suspected that the city administration was giving them a badly constructed building, and that they would be charged a very large sum of money to have it put right.

"We won't take just what they want to give us. It is going to have to last for years and years," said one of them. The Secretary said that if they refused the offered premises or put forward unacceptable conditions, Solidarity would be criticised and smeared as irresponsible. But if, on the other hand, they accepted the premises, they might be given a huge bill for putting everything in order. The chairman summed up the discussion thus: Radom Solidarity will accept the premises offered by the city, but only if the following conditions are fulfilled:
1. The premises should be properly plastered and painted;
2. Heating costs should be at the night tariff;
3. Four telephone lines should be installed at the city's cost;
4. A telex should be installed;
5. Documents guaranteeing the structural solidity of the building should be made available.

How Solidarity is Financed

Like members of unions all over the world, Solidarity's members pay dues, which provide the bulk of the union's income. The old unions had a system of a compulsory one per cent deduction from wages, which provided them with their income. Solidarity has simply inherited that dues structure. The way a worker formally joined Solidarity was to sign a piece of paper for the wage department, authorising the transfer of the one per cent wage deduction to Solidarity. In big plants computerised wage departments simply transferred the cash to Solidarity's bank account. Individual members pay their dues on the same basis of one per cent of salary. One per cent is somewhat higher than the percentage of wages that workers in most of the industrialised democracies pay as union dues. On the basis that Solidarity has up to 10 million members, and assuming an average salary of 5,700 zlotys a month, this would give Solidarity a monthly income, at official exchange rates, of nearly US $17 million of £8.5 million. One does not have to spend very much time in Solidarity offices to know that it simply does not have that amount of money. Many of the less well organised regions do not have an efficient method of collecting members' dues.

Solidarity has had to come to an arrangement with the old unions so that a considerable portion of the dues are used to maintain the wide network of holiday homes, hostels, social and sports clubs that the old unions provided. In some cases Solidarity has taken over the management of these social clubs, but the property, under Polish law, still belongs to the old unions. The division of the money varies slightly from region to region, but roughly 65 per cent remains at plant level, 25 per cent is kept by the region and 10 per cent goes to the national centre at Gdansk.

In terms of Polish currency then, Solidarity is not a poor organisation. It has to pay wages, rent, travel and other costs, but its bank balance is healthily in credit. The trouble is, it cannot buy with zlotys what it mainly needs: good printing equipment, efficient machinery, up-to-date telephone systems and telexes. Nor can it use the zlotys to buy socially needed material, such as modern medical equipment or drugs for hospitals in factories and working-class residential areas. The millions of zlotys are not even much help when it comes to buying food parcels for distribution to needy families. Either such material is not available inside Poland, or the State will not sell it to Solidarity. Solidarity does not have the hard currency to import equipment from the West, and still has to rely on gifts from unions outside Poland for printing equipment and office machinery.

In addition to income from members' dues, Solidarity has raised money by organising public events such as concerts, the proceeds of which go to the union. Some of these events are more an occasion for making contact in public with a wider section of the Polish society than the workers, and are not central to Solidarity's financial needs. One unusual method of raising money for Solidarity was when the Polish Artists' Union held art auctions to which Polish artists either donated or sold for a nominal fee, paintings and sculptures. Two such auctions in Warsaw raised 2.5 million zlotys (US $81,000 — £40,000).

I attended one in Cracow, which was openly advertised with posters around the city. A large hall was packed with a well-dressed, middle-class crowd. The bidding was fast and the prices generous. Some of the paintings seemed of extremely limited quality, and one had a sense of artists thankful, finally, to sell pictures that otherwise would have stayed against a studio wall for many years. But no-one seemed to mind the questionable artistic quality, and several hundred thousand zlotys were raised. The auction was an open public event with many people coming and going.

On 1st May 1981, Solidarity organised showings at Warsaw's cinemas of film reports of the Gdansk strike and other films about Solidarity. The ticket money would be used by Solidarity for social purposes. Similarly, the sale of posters and badges provides Solidarity with a modest income, but is more important as a means of visibly spreading the new union's presence.

Plant . . . Region . . . National

In the reception hall of the Solidarity office in Warsaw, there is a chart on the wall which purports to show the organisational structure of Solidarity. Like all charts outlining trade union structures, it is neat and purposeful, with each level of union organisation leading on to the next. In real unions, as in real life, organisation and structure is never that neat. Solidarity has an overlapping structure in which personalities and power bases play an important role. In Szczecin, for example, the leadership of one shipyard, the Warski shipyard, and the leadership of the region overlap considerably; so much so, that Bogdan Batura, a Warski welder, complained to me in May 1981, that he was worried about the level of union organisation in the shipyard because so many of the key people had to spend all their time on regional affairs. Although workers are everywhere in the majority on Solidarity's committees, there are a large number of intellectuals, especially teachers and post-graduate students, who have played an important role since August 1980. As Solidarity becomes more institutionalised, it is less and less easy to fit them into the trade union structure.

The official Solidarity structure shows a three tier level. At the bottom is the plant or workplace, followed by the region, followed by the national level. It all works on a system of direct and indirect democracy. In big plants, workers are divided up into "circles", groups of up to fifty workers belonging to the same area of the plant. They elect a "delegate" to an assembly of delegates, which then elects a chairperson, a praesidium, and the various subcommittees needed to deal with matters like health and safety, holiday home allocations, sports and social facilities and finance. The size of the praesidium varies from plant to plant. In many plants workers have elected white collar or professional staff on to the praesidium. At the Unitra factory in Wroclaw, for example, the chairman is a design engineer and his deputy is an economist. In Cracow, I was told that despite efforts to push forward manual workers for nomination to leadership positions, in many cases workers "are still nominating the better qualified people in the plants".

Late in 1980 Solidarity in Szczecin circulated this leaflet to all plants where elections were taking place. "Think carefully before nominating a candidate and before voting. Have you observed the behaviour of your candidate in the workplace? Is he someone who always listens carefully to what you say before expressing his own opinion? Is he capable of representing your interests in a firm and uncompromising manner when facing up to the management? Remember that if the best of us — honest, brave, firm and wedded to the great ideas of solidarity and social justice — are elected, then the great hope of the Polish summer will be realised. Remember that the presence of irresponsible people in the union leadership can slow down the process of renewal, and disappoint our expectations. Think carefully! If your candidate is a member of a political organisation, ask yourself if he is not taking advantage of the election to obtain new benefits and privileges, or if he will really serve the ideals of the working class? Think carefully! Do not let yourself be swayed by momentary sympathy. Don't let yourself be taken in by cheap and seductive speeches! Choose those who will not let you down."

Solidarity's concern that it might be infiltrated by elements under Communist Party control does not seem to have much foundation. In Silesia, there was crude anti-Solidarity propaganda circulated at the time of elections in the key strongholds of the mines. One of the leaflets showed a crude cartoon of a grasping hand, each fingertip of which had the face of a leading local Solidarity activist, and beside it a line describing him as a "drunkard" or a hooligan and other insults.

The ploy did not work, as candidates known to be anti-party in Silesia were elected overwhelmingly. Party membership was usually irrelevant in Solidarity elections. Usually it was a case of Solidarity infiltrating the Party rather than the other way round. At plant level, there have been changes in the composition of the Solidarity leadership since the first group of people were elected on an *ad hoc* basis during and after August 1980. The average age of plant praesidiums went up slightly after the formal plant elections were held in December 1980-February 1981. Some did not have the staying power and dropped out: some were rejected when the formal plant elections were held. The first few months of Solidarity's existence was a kind of probationary period for its leaders. In most cases, they have succeeded in continuing to keep the workers' confidence and, most people in Solidarity agree, three-quarters of Solidarity's current leadership at plant level consists of those who emerged in the early weeks.

Solidarity had hoped to organise its regional elections for early in 1981, but the succession of crises that confronted the union during the winter, coupled with the immense organisational problems involved in holding regional elections, meant that they were put off until early Summer 1981. A union defines itself by holding democratic elections, and Solidarity was very conscious of the need not to shuffle along with the *ad hoc* regional committees dating from the formative period.

The regional elections threw up considerable problems for Solidarity. How does one combine steelworkers, bus drivers, teachers and hotel clerks into an electoral system that is fair, democratic and representative? In the giant Mazowsze region, which includes Warsaw and the area around the capital, the organisation of the elections has been a considerable headache for Janusz Kondrasiak, a member of the regional praesidium and Anatol Lawina, a computer expert trained by IBM in Vienna, who heads the group dealing with the technical organisation of the elections.

The object was to produce a regional assembly on the basis of one delegate per 1,000 members. The electoral constituencies were formed in three ways: firstly, big factories with more than 1,000 members; secondly, areas based on 1,000 members gathered from different workplaces within the same industry or profession — Warsaw hotels form such an electoral area; thirdly, on a territorial basis — in one Warsaw suburb, the electoral area is composed of a school, a research institute and a metal factory.

Obviously, there were tensions in composing the electoral areas as people tried to make certain that their composition would ensure the election of a favoured candidate. Lawina (who is not a candidate) said: "People are afraid of being manipulated. We have not had open elections in Poland for 35 years. People want their own interests represented and supported by the region. There may well be clashes between the sectoral interest of a plant or a group of workers and the interests of the region as a whole. Workers have different demands, different priorities, not all of which can be satisfied".

Once the electoral areas are decided, an electoral college is formed based on a ratio of 1 member per 20 or 50 voters. It is that electoral college which chooses the regional assembly delegate, who will hold office for two years. The regional assemblies met in mid-July 1981, and decided upon a regional President, the size of the regional praesidium, and the number and scope of sub-committees. Solidarity hoped to be in a position to organise a national congress for the end of August to coincide with the signing of the Gdansk

Agreement in 1980. The voting in Solidarity elections for delegates, chairpersons and committee members is by secret ballot at the meeting where the candidates are discussed.

National Committee and Executive

The national leadership of Solidarity formed itself on 17th September 1980, when representatives of 33 Regional Interfactory Founding Committees met in Gdansk. They unanimously elected Lech Walesa as chairman of the National Co-ordinating Commission, which consists of the chairmen of all regional Solidarities. This body in turn, elected a small national praesidium, which has provided the effective day-to-day national leadership of Solidarity ever since. The National Co-ordinating Commission meets once every fourteen days, though more often if needed. With more than fifty participants, regional chairmen, plus advisers and experts, it can give the impression of being more of a convention than a well-ordered and disciplined trade union leadership taking decisions of great importance for the country. The debates at the National Co-ordinating Commission are recorded on cassette recorders and taken back by regional representatives to be played locally. Extracts of the discussions are also carried in many Solidarity journals. The meeting offers a regular opportunity for regional leaders to exchange experiences and ideas and to keep in touch with what is happening in different parts of Poland. There can be no doubt that the National Co-ordinating Commission's decisions are representative. Each time it has called a short national general strike in order to demonstrate its strength to the government over a particular issue the strike order has been 100 per cent obeyed.

Behind the National Co-ordinating Commission lies the National Praesidium consisting of Lech Walesa, Andrzej Gwiazda and Bogdan Lis from Gdansk, four other members from Solidarity's most important regions and three national advisers. There is also an 11-strong so-called "organisation committee" which prepares the National Co-ordinating Commission meeting and which has great influence. It is Praesidium members who lead the negotiations with the government. During the crisis over the Bydgoszcz incident in March 1981, a threatened all-out general strike was called off by Lech Walesa and some members of Praesidium without convening a meeting of the National Co-ordinating Commission. The exact powers and the relationship between the Praesidium and the National Co-ordinating Commission and the power and relationship of both bodies with Solidarity's national chairman, Lech Walesa, will be one of the major organisational problems Solidarity has to tackle after its national congress has convened.

Another hang-over from the dislike of the old unions is that of having too many full-time employees, too many trade union bureaucrats and office personnel. That feeling was particularly evident in the first months of Solidarity's existence, when questions about the shortage of secretaries and clerks to type, file and maintain the necessary office routines to serve hundreds of thousands of members, were shrugged off with remarks about not becoming office-dominated and bureaucratised like the old unions.

A Fabian Society pamphlet published in 1900 explains that the reason why workers need full-time officials is that they thus pay someone who can speak up for their interests and can confront employers without fear of dismissal or victimisation. That theory, which is still the underlying logic of having full-time union officials paid for by workers' subscriptions, does not apply in Poland, where there is only one employer. In fact, the majority of full-time Solidarity leaders and activists are on paid leave from their workplace and are not paid directly by the union. Under Polish law, the old unions were allowed one full-time official per 1000 members and Solidarity has simply inherited that practice. Its continuation is one of Solidarity's demands in the new trade union bill it was discussing with the government in 1981. There are increasing numbers of people on the Solidarity payroll. In Warsaw there are 100 full-time employees, while there are only seventeen in Szczecin. In many regions lawyers are paid for part-time work in taking up individual cases on Solidarity's behalf.

Watching one of Solidarity's highly-qualified international affairs specialists turn from involved and delicate discussion about a foreign delegation's visit to do some simple copy-typing of 'thank you' letters in Spanish for Lech Walesa to sign, I wondered if it was the best use of her time. But Solidarity is still reluctant to hire too many secretaries for their officials. Andrzej Zabinski, in his speech to the police in Katowice, about how to weaken Solidarity, clearly understood the potential for corrupting the new union: "They have to get a taste of power. We have to make quarters and meeting places available to them, and equip them with every luxury. I don't know many who would not get corrupted by power — it is simply a matter of time and degree."

Inside plants Solidarity keeps in touch with members through a process of permanent consultation. Weekly meetings of work section representatives are held, while praesidium members are easily approachable in the rooms set aside for Solidarity inside factories. Solidarity regions, in turn, bring together factory representatives for regular discussions at the regional level. These meetings serve to keep members in touch with what their representatives are saying and thinking at plant, regional and national levels.

Solidarity's organisation and structure has developed from the way in which the new union came into being and as a reaction against what the workers saw as the failings of the old unions. Most trade union organisation grows slowly, and many Western trade union leaders will reckon on a minimum of five years between the launch of a re-organisation or re-structuring idea and its final acceptance and implementation. Solidarity developed its embryo structure, with its particular emphasis on organisation on a regional, rather than industrial basis, within weeks. So far, it has stood up to what has been demanded of it and it has been able to grow and develop according to the needs of Poland's workers.

If Solidarity can maintain the regional commitment of strong groups of workers to help weak groups, even at the expense of their own wage levels; if Solidarity can maintain its policy of maximum democracy and consultation when the novelty of endless meetings wears off; if Solidarity can ensure that praesidiums, or even chairmen, do not consider themselves more knowledgeable and thus equipped to take important decisions without reference to wider bodies; if Solidarity can keep track of its letters and files without developing an office bureaucracy that freezes out the rank and file member; if Solidarity can improve the quality of its premises and working conditions without losing the welcoming shabbiness in which no worker, currently, feels out of place; if Solidarity can concentrate on major economic and social questions at national, regional and plant level, without diminishing its current availability to a myriad of individual complaints, many of them far removed from traditional trade union matters; if Solidarity over the next few years can do all or some of these things, then it will have done something that most unions have not been able to do in the past. But that is an awful lot of "ifs". Developing an organisational system, that can permanently handle 8-10 million members both efficiently and with political sensitivity, remains one of Solidarity's key tasks.

Chapter 7

Solidarity's Achievements

Drawing up a balance sheet of Solidarity's achievements since August 1980 presents problems from a Western trade unionist's viewpoint. The classical definition of a trade union sees it as a combination of workers existing to defend and improve living standards — principally through the mechanism of securing wage increases, longer holidays and shorter hours. Most people's ideas about trade unionism, fashioned as they are to a great extent by the media, revolve around the economic activities of unions. Strikes usually have to do with workers' bids to get a fairer share of the wealth they create. A union is judged by the success with which it can obtain financial benefits for its members.

In Poland, by contrast, when I posed the question endlessly to workers in many different industries: "What has Solidarity done for you? What difference has it made to your life? What do you consider to be its main achievements?", I can check back through hundreds of pages of notes and not once did I receive the reply that Solidarity has won a wage increase. The need for more cash to compensate the increase in food costs that sparked off the Polish summer of 1980 became virtually forgotten as workers rapidly moved on to make wider demands and to claim victories that had little to do with wages.

A sense of gaining some power over their own lives, both at work and in society, is perhaps the best way of describing the change that Solidarity has brought about for individual workers. In Katowice a 33-year-old welder put it this way in December 1980: "We have been dismantling social and political collectives: the Party, the Youth Movement, other Party controlled organisations. These had tremendous power — promotions, cars, apartments were all obtained through them. Now we have stopped the arbitrary distribution of apartments. We are being consulted about changes in the plants. We are making management take responsibility as individuals for their plants".

The desire for more efficient management is a common one inside Solidarity. After an initial refusal to meet Solidarity representatives most managers were persuaded that it was better to consult the newly elected workers' representatives. In Elblag, near the Baltic coast, the local Solidarity office was in a shopping arcade, and Solidarity used the shop windows to place criticisms of local managers who refused to meet Solidarity representatives. "Sometimes, we just told a manager that he might appear in the window and, very quickly, he became willing to meet us and discuss our grievances," explained Ryszard Kalinowski, the Solidarity chairman in Elblag.

An example of mismanagement was given by Maciek Stolwiski, a turner at the Ursus tractor factory in Warsaw. "Materials would often be over-ordered and then stored in the open air without proper protection and, thus, were ruined. Machinists would be given disproportionately large pieces of metal from which to make small cylinders and there was considerable waste as they ground away the excess metal. Assembly lines were often halted because parts did not arrive in time. We have set up a special commission which is examining all these examples of waste with careful documentation. In fact, Solidarity is already having an effect as workers simply refuse to perform a job in the old, highly inefficient way," said Stolwiski.

In Szczecin there were similar complaints about management inefficiency. "They appointed people who did not know what they were doing," declared 58-year-old Alexander Krystosikia, a plumber at the Parnica Ship Repair Yard. "Frankly we haven't got an answer to that problem. To obtain materials or to get something done you had to know the right people, or else you bullied those below you, or you crawled up to your superiors."

Since August 1980 that relationship has altered, though Solidarity activists have learnt that production problems cannot all be blamed on inefficient or lazy management. The crippling shortage of hard currency or poor ordering in the past has meant that whole areas of the Polish economy are disabled because of the absence of a key raw material or essential parts from the West.

In some cases pressure from Solidarity has led to the dismissal of managers. I was told that in Wroclaw more than one hundred managers had resigned in the three months following the creation of Solidarity. At the Huta Warszawa steel plant in Warsaw, by contrast, there had been no significant managerial changes by early Summer 1981. The rolling of managerial heads was not seen in most areas to be the answer. Sometimes workers bypassed managers. Szczecin Solidarity spoke directly to the Solidarity office in Czestochowa in order to obtain a vital supply of tin to permit the continued working of certain factories in Szczecin. Everywhere managers were under pressure to act in a less arbitrary way. The issuing of individual bonuses — a key tool in the management armoury all over the world, as it permits the manager to favour one worker over another and thereby ensure the former's loyalty — was made a public affair with the names of those receiving a bonus pin-

ned up on the notice board in many factories. Victimisation became
almost impossible. It was not just that workers could take their case
to Solidarity but managers simply did not try it on, as they knew
the ensuing row would not be worth the effort of trying to get rid of
someone they did not like.

Health and Safety

Along with inefficient production, a major complaint of Polish
workers is the poor level of health, safety and hygiene standards in
factories. Industrial safety and the working environment has only
really become a major trade union issue in the past twenty years.
The more crudely obvious dangers in the work processes and the
cancer- or disease-inducing substances and chemicals may have
been banned, but workers are still exposed to dangers in the work
place, including high noise levels, fumes, dust, mineral fibres,
solvents, sprays, paints, as well as many different kinds of
dangerous machinery. Often the effect of these substances is not
apparent until later in life, long after the worker can secure compensation or make the employer stop using the substance or hazar-
dous process. For most of this century no-one took much notice of
the dangers caused by asbestos, but American medical researchers
now reckon that 2 million Americans will die because they worked
with or handled asbestos, whose tiny fibres cause cancer-provoking
lesions in the linings of the lungs and stomach.

To protect workers against dangerous substances or work
methods costs money, and can slow down production rates, and so
employers have only been prepared to protect workers under strong
trade union pressure, or when forced to by government legislation.
In theory, Polish law permits a worker to refuse to perform a job
he or she considers unsafe or dangerous for health or safety
reasons. But this law was (and still is) widely ignored, especially as
the piece rate system common in Poland's manufacturing industry
needs to have production interrupted as little as possible. In the
Warski shipyard in Szczecin, workers have changing and shower
facilities and everyone is obliged to wear a safety helmet. But according to Bogdan Batura, a Warski welder, workers have to operate
in unsafe conditions. "We don't have enough protective clothes,
especially masks. Painters would be spraying in one area of a ship
and nearby other workers would be doing other work without face
masks. The fumes from the paint are highly dangerous and often
workers would be poisoned by the paint fumes. Often welders have
to work in extremely confined or narrow spaces and they don't
always have direct extraction equipment to suck away fumes from
the point of the operation. The masks welders wear come from the
Soviet Union and are made out of a cloth material. They become

very dirty," he said.

Steelworker Jacek Lipinski, Solidarity's safety officer at the Huta Warszawa plant near Warsaw, although talking to me six months after I had interviewed Batura, agreed with his Szczecin colleague. "Health and safety has been one of our greatest problems for many years. The health and safety representatives of the old unions were too close to management. The health and safety councils were worthless. Production had to be kept up at all costs. Research on health and safety always boasted of steady improvements, and reports claimed that working conditions were idyllic."

Since the arrival of Solidarity the official accident rate has shot up. Lipinski does not believe that there are more accidents, but that every small accident is now being recorded whereas, in the past, workers would simply shrug their shoulders and forget about it because reporting the accident achieved nothing. In addition, managers received a special bonus if they could show a good safety record. "Now *all* the accidents are being recorded. Before they were covered up, but foremen and managers are now nervous and insist that even the smallest scratch is recorded; everything is registered. In the first three months of 1981 there were 2,000 serious accidents in the steel industry. Here in Huta Warszawa there is very poor protection against fumes, which is one of our big problems. In the worst places there is some kind of ventilation, but it would need a huge investment for the plant to be made as safe as we would like it to be," Lipinski said.

The need to get the money to pay for health and safety protection, like the need to find foreign currency to purchase essential raw materials and parts from abroad in order to maintain production, is a hurdle that the mere existence of Solidarity does not overcome. Important changes have been made. At Huta Wasrszawa Solidarity is devising a system of rotation for workers in jobs that are known to be dangerous. Previously workers had stayed doing the same dangerous job on a permanent basis. Another important gain for workers, the abolition of compulsory overtime, has important health and safety implications, as workers doing extra work at the end of a tiring shift are more likely to make mistakes that lead to accidents.

Problems Outside the Workplace

At most times of the day in the major Polish cities one can always see the sad sight of a queue of people waiting in a Solidarity reception hall with their problems which they hope Solidarity can solve. Of course the new union has not been able to solve all the problems dumped in its lap, but the fact that it is there and available to act as an independent and powerful force in Polish society has given the population hope, and represents a major breakthrough in any East European society. The problems brought to Solidarity's regional offices are often simple individual cases. In Katowice, Kazimierz Switon cited two cases he had had to deal with on the day I met him: "I have just had to find a place in the mountains for a 12 year-old girl with pneumonia, and another problem just given to me is what to do with a juvenile delinquent whose father has just left home and whose mother is very ill". Many individuals come to Solidarity asking for cases that they consider were unfairly handled by the authorities in previous years to be taken up again. One should not accept the crude anti-communist caricature which depicts Soviet bloc countries living under a monolithic, centrally-directed state which denies the citizen any chance of success against the bureaucracy. The different organisations that existed in Poland to represent social groups such as peasants, veterans, workers, young people as well as the various party and regional groupings, allowed a certain margin for playing one set of decision makers off against another. But the consequence of there being ultimately only one source of authentic power — the Party — meant that attempts to secure justice or to emerge the winner in a struggle with any of the power holders at a local or a regional level could only be finessed so far through the system before coming to a dead stop. Before August 1980, the Party was not everything, but it was the final arbiter. Now that too has changed. Regional officials are obliged to negotiate with Solidarity on a wide range of issues. In many regions bus routes and schedules have been reorganised at Solidarity's request. In Silesia an important aluminium smelter was closed down because of the disastrous effect it was having on the local environment.

One of the major discussion points between Solidarity and the regional authorities has been over food distribution and availability. Given Poland's disastrous food shortage, the regional authorities cannot always provide Solidarity with the answers it wishes to hear. Three weeks before Christmas 1980 I listened to a Solidarity Praesidium meeting in Radom, where the question of negotiations with the Voivod over the all-important Christmas meat ration was debated.

— "We need to have 2 kilos of meat and 2 kilos of sausage. We cannot give up more than half a kilo of meat and the sausage ration must be kept up."
— "Yes, but supposing he offers only 1 kilo of meat?"
— "But our children are already starving, we cannot let them starve any longer."
— "But if he only offers 1 kilo of meat?"

— "We break off discussion and tell him to stop exporting meat from the region."

The chairman then comes in.

— "You must insist on 2 kilos of meat. But maybe we could take 200 grams less."

— "No, you can't do that. The workers have insisted on 2 kilos. You must go back to them."

— "OK," says the chairman, "It's agreed. The Voivod will be told that he cannot go below 2 kilos of meat and 2 kilos of sausage without reference back to the workers."

At Christmas time the government did manage to find extra supplies of meat to provide enough for most families to enjoy the festivities. The constant pressure of Solidarity meant that decisions on distribution were now taken with more care for their impact on the population.

In many cases regional officials have been removed as a result of pressure by Solidarity. Strikes in Czestochowa and Jelenia-Gora led to resignations of local officials. At the national level nearly 30 ministerial posts have been reshuffled since August 1980, including two Prime Ministers who have come and gone. Much of this reflects the struggle for power inside the Communist Party and the search for people who can handle the extraordinary political, economic and social pressures released in Poland by the creation of Solidarity. But to the average worker who is a member of the new union, it is a tribute to the power of Solidarity that so many, hitherto untouchable senior people are being made to resign and, in some cases, being forced publicly to account for themselves or even stand trial for past malpractices.

Day-to-Day Life

Well below the national or regional level Solidarity is making a difference to the day-to-day life of the worker. In most plants there are now joint Solidarity-management committees that look after housing allocation, medical care, pension allocation, as well as the sport and recreation clubs, and that are organised on a workplace basis. Communist social organisation places far more emphasis on providing services or leisure via the workplace rather than external community organised or oriented provision of services. Hospitals and medical centres, for example, are often part of, or attached to, large plants. Paradoxically this has given Solidarity a much stronger position in society than, say, a West European union which does not have to handle so many social problems in the context of workplace organisation. A woman electrician in Warsaw gave a specific example of the difference Solidarity was making. She sat on a joint committee in her factory which dealt with the allocation of holiday places. "We want to build and develop proper holiday centres. At the moment we have to find places in hotels or private homes by the seaside. But there are not enough places and we ought to have our own holiday centre. Renting rooms in private houses is not satisfactory. The party and the militia have plenty of buildings which serve no useful purpose. We should be able to take them over. At least we have reorganised the way holiday places are allocated. Before, the holidays only went to the "right" people, those who were favoured by the management, the old official union or the factory Party branch. Now it is done with justice. Each section of the factory gets a defined number of places which must be distributed fairly, even though that presents problems as there are just not enough holiday places to go round."

To the rank and file worker, then, Solidarity has changed and improved the quality of life in ways which wage rises cannot express. Again and again workers will tell you: "The atmosphere is much better," or "We now really feel as if we are owners of our workplace," or "Before, if you complained, they shouted at you. Now you say what you like." The mere existence of Solidarity has forced through changes in workplace and social relations which add up, in the words of Warsaw University sociologist Jacek Kurczewski, a member of Solidarity's commission of twenty-five expert advisers, to: "Something like Britain's 1688 Glorious Revolution — that is to say, an event that produces revolutionary changes in society, and does so without violence."

All this sounds positive and optimistic. However, Polish workers themselves caution against imagining that, because they now have an organisation that can stand up for them, the nature of work, boring, dirty, sometimes dangerous, usually monotonous, has changed. In addition, the nine months since August 1980 have not required Solidarity to make any decisions connected with economic reform (mainly because the government had delayed introducing an economic reform package) which might call for unemployment or a reduction in workers' purchasing power. Once that policy is embarked upon, the traditional trade union demands of income defence and improvement, as well as job protection, could come to the fore again, especially from the industrial section of Solidarity's membership. The mere existence of Solidarity has not brought about improvements in the two key areas of industrial production and economic growth, and of food production and distribution. But there has, nonetheless, been a qualitative improvement in the life of Polish workers. Before, if they had a case or a cause there was no outlet if either conflicted with prevailing ideology or bureaucratic sluggishness. Now they have an effective tribune — Solidarity. In the words of the woman electrician who, for the first time in her life was seeing holiday places allocated fairly, "It's difficult to sum up exactly what difference Solidarity has made for me, but now I feel free".

Chapter 8

Economic Reform —
Is Self-Management the Answer?

The Polish economy was bad enough in the Summer of 1980. By the middle of 1981 it was verging on disaster. Even with the queues and inflationary pressure of 1980 there were goods in the stores and food was available. Nine months later, most of the staple Polish foods — meat, butter, sugar, cooking oil, cereal and flour — were rationed and in extremely short supply. It was difficult even to find cigarettes. Exports had slumped. Two hundred and fifty million dollars worth of coal, normally exported to West Germany for precious hard currency, had simply not been dug out of the pits. Polish workers were clocking in for work each morning but it was reckoned that 25 per cent of the country's productive capacity was lying idle because of shortages of raw materials, energy, spare parts or components that needed unavailable foreign currency. This was the first time that there had been such an economic slump in Poland since the war. In capitalist countries, industrial production would decline as sharply only in the event of a depression even worse than the one engendered in recent years. Investment programmes in Poland came to a dead halt. The economic recession in the West did not help matters and there was an obvious reluctance by Western investors to put new money into Poland while the political situation remained so unstable. Poland's immediate neighbours in Eastern Europe also slowed down trade as a result of the political uncertainty. All this had an effect on Solidarity. In August 1980 workers still felt as if they were needed. Nine months later the spectre of unemployment was looming. Wladyslaw Gomulka, Poland's leader from 1956 – 70, was said to be boasting in his retirement villa not far from Warsaw, that even under his much (and justly) maligned economic rule the Polish economy had never stopped growing, however unevenly.

Agriculture suffered from a run of bad luck. The 1980 harvest was one of the worst in post-war years. The crop of potatoes was down by half. In 1980 there were 200,000 peasants who wanted to buy tractors, who had the money to buy the tractors, but no tractors were available. Gierek's policy of investment in heavy industry meant that the steel needed to build tractors was diverted to building new industrial or chemical plants. Even the government's attempt to appease the peasants by raising State prices for agricultural produce — the price paid for a litre of milk went up from 6.5 zlotys to 14 zlotys, for example — meant only that the peasants had more money in their pockets, not that there was anything to spend it on. The massive wage increases won by workers after August 1980 have been of little use to them, as there has been nothing to buy with the newly gained cash. Solidarity economists reckon that one third of the population's purchasing power is simply not being used, thus removing up to 500 billion zlotys from the economy because of the lack of commodities to buy.

While facing a disastrous internal economic situation Poland has had to juggle with a growing external debt which in June 1981 stood at US $27 billion. Some Western commentators, dazzled by the sheer enormity of the figures involved, have tended to make the resolution of the interest payment and capital repayment of this debt the central question in the Polish economy. Certainly the Poles have tried hard to get the debt rescheduled and repayment either deferred or slowed down. They have been successful with Western governments and have also persuaded the four hundred private banks that have lent Poland money to be reasonably generous — generous, that is, by bankers' standards! Western bankers have little choice over Poland. To insist too strongly on rigorous repayments is to risk Poland defaulting, which would bring down a whole edifice of East European credit that, in turn, would have potentially explosive consequences for the world banking and credit system. Although the Polish external debt is large, there are other countries which, on a per capita basis, have a larger debt without having the unending sense of crisis that surrounds the Polish debt.

The Polish economy is   highly centralised with fifteen State ministries controlling the key industries. The crucial agricultural economy is largely in private hands — about three million small plots of land — but distribution is centrally controlled. Poland has never been able to settle on a stable agricultural policy. Torn between communist dislike of private ownership of land and the Polish peasants' stubborn refusal to give up their tiny plots of land (most are smaller than the minimum acreage considered by Western agricultural economists to be necessary for viable farming) the different Polish governments after the war have chopped and changed the direction of agricultural policy. Forced collectivisation was stopped by Gomulka, while Gierek abolished the compulsory delivery of agricultural produce in 1972. The carrot has been matched with the stick, however, and the State made it very difficult for private farmers to obtain the three essentials for small scale farming — agricultural credits, tractors and other farm machinery and fertilisers. The government also offered farmers derisory pensions if they would agree to leave their land to the State, but this provoked suspicion and resentment amongst a peasant population for whom the right to leave land to succeeding generations was a cherished part of their tradition. The government naturally favoured State farms and the State-run enterprises providing agricultural services. Although representing 25 per cent of the agricultural economy, these State organisations were allocated 70 per cent of State expenditure on agricultural investment.

The Hungarian Model

According to one of Solidarity's leading economic advisers, Tadeusz Kowalik, Poland cannot move towards fully collectivised agriculture for deep-rooted political, historical and psychological reasons. Kowalik also argues that, for similar reasons, Polish industry cannot have disciplined centralised planning. Unlike East Germany or Czechoslovakia, where prior to 1939 there was a developed and relatively advanced capitalist system with efficient managerial systems and disciplined workforces, pre-war Poland was a backward industrial country without the managerial talent available to run the centralised economy imposed after 1945.

In Hungary, by contrast, the State, after it had gone through the trauma of 1956, settled for a much more decentralised economy. Enterprises were given great autonomy to decide prices and to reduce or increase workforces. Some foreign trade monopolies were even broken. The government laid down broad planning frameworks within which enterprises could operate.

The Hungarian model is just one of the many possibilities of economic reform for Poland that Solidarity economists have been discussing since the creation of the union. The need for an economic reform package was agreed in the Gdansk negotiations between the strikers and Vice-Premier Jagielski. Point 6 of the Gdansk Agreement stated: "We consider it essential to speed up the preparation of an economic reform. The authorities will work out and publish the basic principles of such a reform in the next few months. Only a society which has a firm grasp of reality can take the initiative in reforming the economy. The government will significantly increase the areas of socio-economic information to which society, the trade unions, and other social and economic organisations have access". As with so many other parts of the Gdansk Agreement the Polish government failed to keep its word through a swift introduction of economic reform, though the recognition and registration of Rural Solidarity was seen as a major step forward in moving towards properly negotiated agricultural reforms. A government commission was set up, but its first reports produced early in 1981 were dismissed by Solidarity economist Ryszard Bugaj as being without much substance. In fact, the government was faced with an unenviable task. The men who had been responsible for the disastrous economic mismanagement in the 1970's were now being asked to sit in judgement upon themselves. Although several ministers had been removed and more than one thousand government and party officials were under investigation on charges of economic mismanagement or corruption, men like Kania and Jagielski, (who was now in charge of the economy), had been side by side with Gierek during the previous decade. The second problem hampering government willingness to suggest far-reaching economic reform was the lack of political stability within the party. To implement the kind of reform necessary to stabilise the Polish economy would need sweeping institutional reform which could only be achieved by a strong leadership. The intense struggle inside the party during all 1981 meant a complete lack of the necessary political cohesion to push through economic reforms.

Although the government set up a joint commission with Solidarity to discuss economic reform, Bugaj was complaining in May 1981 that the Solidarity representatives were not being given enough information upon which to base decisions. Broadly speaking, Solidarity sees economic reform going in the following direction. There should be a high degree of independence in price and labour policy for enterprises, which should be allowed to combine together on a voluntary, not a compulsory, basis. State ministries and lower-level supervisory bodies to cover particular sectors should be abolished and the State's role should be exercised through functional ministries such as Finance, Planning, Trade. Self-management of enterprises through the creation of workers' councils, which would be quite independent of Solidarity, should be encouraged. Price reform should aim at creating the production of goods based upon a greater sensitivity to market forces (with certain exceptions, in both prices and products) in order to get a much clearer idea of how the economy is moving. Wages should be fixed with a maximum 8 – 1 spread between lowest and highest incomes. As a general rule the government should not directly compel enterprises to produce specific products; if the government does insist on the production of a loss-making product, it should compensate the firm concerned.

It might sound like a plausible economic package, but it is fraught with potentially problematic consequences. To dismantle State supervision of industries would mean 200,000 functionaries losing their jobs. The jobs are well paid, most of the affected people are Party members, and are unlikely to encourage tendencies in the Party that will lead to their losing their jobs. If one takes into consideration their families and dependents this is close on one million people who would be affected by this aspect of economic reform. Solidarity too, faces unemployment problems arising from any implementation of real economic reform. Talking to steel workers in Warsaw I was told that they accepted the need for a reduction in the labour force at the Huta Warszawa steel plant, especially if the plant was modernised, but they expected all the people to be made redundant to have the opportunity for retraining. One member of the Praesidium chipped in to say that redundant workers should be made to go and work on the land, as Poland's agricultural workforce has a high average age. He was rounded on by his colleagues, who told him that it was impossible for Solidarity to direct labour in that fashion. Tadeusz Kowalik is not so pessimistic about the prospect of large scale unemployment amongst Poland's industrial workers as a result of economic reforms. He believes that factory managers will still keep a certain number of workers on their books as a labour reserve, and that the deep-rooted social commitment against unemployment will lessen the possibilities of the kind of mass closures and lay-offs that are a feature of the recession in Western economies. He also believes that the government could introduce positive measures, such as expanding Poland's diminutive service sector, in order to increase the total number of jobs, and even reducing working time if necessary. "Full employment, as one of the fundamental socialist principles of Poland, has to remain something to which Solidarity is fully committed." he said.

Self-Management and Workers' Control

One of the biggest debates that has continued inside Solidarity since its foundation has been over self-management, or workers' control of plants. The debate has followed the classic divisions between those who argue that workers and their unions must stay aloof from economic and managerial decision-making and simply act to defend workers' interests when they are under threat, and those who argue that workers should be involved in the decisions that affect their lives before those decisions are made, and not merely come in to react against the management decisions when it is too late. Although workers' councils were first legislated for in Poland in 1945, there is a great deal of suspicion over plant level committees after the failure of the workers' councils set up as part of the Polish 'October' of 1956 – 57. During that period, rather than create separate trade unions the Polish workers elected workers' councils that had a double role as co-managers of the plant and problem-solvers on behalf of workers.

The workers' councils set up in 1956 were tolerated for little more than twelve months before Gomulka made them subordinate to the official power structure at factory level, as part of his crackdown in 1958. The collective memory of workers' councils is that they are no substitute for an independent trade union and that they could be too easily incorporated and rendered impotent. At the same time the creation of Solidarity was not enough to guarantee a renewal of the economy.

From an early stage, workers and leaders of Solidarity were discussing the idea of self-management at the enterprise level. In November 1980, Tadeusz Mazowiecki, one of Solidarity's chief advisers, wrote: "We will also be led to reform workers' self-management which can no longer keep its present form, and to discuss the efficiency of workers' control of the enterprises. It is clear that the union cannot accept the responsibility for the system of economic management; it is not prepared to assume this type of responsibility and, above all, that is not its role. But it cannot remain indifferent with regard to the economic situation, nor to the application of necessary reforms.

When I visited a small electrical factory (2,000 employees) in Wroclaw in December 1980, the chairman of the factory's Solidarity unit, a 49-year-old computer data supervisor, Radoslaw Obst, told me that he was interested in involving workers jointly with management in trying to resolve the problems in the factory. He wanted to know about the West German system of industrial democracy. "We need to look at the products we are producing and the prices we are charging. After all, we are co-owners of this plant under our system. We should be visiting the best plants and asking ourselves why we can't produce as efficiently as they do. Our biggest problem over the next six months (remember this interview was carried out in December 1980 — *author's note)* will be to implement economic reforms at all levels. Here we are desperately short of information. It is still difficult to express the solutions as we see them," he said.

Six months later Solidarity was still waiting for the government's economic reform package. At the Warsaw steel plant of Huta Warszawa, members of the plant praesidium were divided on the question of plant self-management. Some said that Solidarity should keep away from all suggestion of joint responsibility for running the plant. Others argued that it would be acceptable, provided a workers' council had real power — the power, for example, to dismiss unsatisfactory managers. At Huta Warsawa they would be willing to operate a system of self-management to lay down exact production plans, both in quantity and type of steel produced, plant capacity, and investment programmes. But only on condition that they had real power within any self-management scheme.

Tadeusz Kowalik believes that the workers' control union independence circle can be squared by completely separating the two
functions. Workers' councils would be elected by the whole
workforce, irrespective of trade union affiliation, while Solidarity
would continue to operate in a traditional trade union fashion and
not be directly involved in the sharing of managerial power at plant
level. It sounds fine in theory, but the West German experience suggests that inevitably trade unions get drawn into workers' council
elections and are obliged to run a trade union slate in order to
maintain their effective presence amongst the workers.

The Crisis Ahead

Some Solidarity economists say that the leaders of Solidarity do not
have enough understanding of economic theory and practice to
handle the economic policies and decisions that have confronted
Poland since August 1980. In fact most Solidarity leaders will
argue, and rightly so in my view, that the Polish economic crisis
cannot be solved outside the framework of a general political settlement. The importance of the supremacy of politics over economic
objectives is well illustrated by what has happened in Poland since
August 1980. Had the Solidarity members stopped and considered
the enormity of the economic crisis into which the country was in-
exorably heading, it is difficult to believe that they would have
made the organisational and other gains that they have achieved.
Nine months into the life of the new union the two sides — government and Solidarity — had still not managed to find common
ground for economic reform. The fault lay squarely with the
government which knew — and had tacitly accepted by signing the
Gdansk Agreement — that Polish workers demanded certain major
reforms in the country's political, economic and social structures
before they would be willing to agree to a permanent settlement
that would permit the economy to get moving again. An essential
part of any economic return would be an increase in prices (and
after 1970, 1976 and 1980, price increases are a sensitive subject in
Poland!) and the acceptance of job losses, however prettily the latter were dressed up. To ask workers and their union, anywhere in
the world, voluntarily to embrace both a decline in real living standards and in total employment is to put in question the very reason
that trade unions came into existence. Solidarity was willing to
swallow this in return for real and lasting changes in the organisation of Polish society. In particular it knew that the roll-call of
ministers and officials who had been sacked meant very little.
Changing names was pointless if the institutional structure of
economic decision making remained the same, and if workers con-

tinued to be excluded. The Polish working class had shown by August 1980 that it was no longer prepared to live with the kind of economic system developed by the Polish Communist Party. The quest for a system of economic management that corresponds to Polish workers' and Polish society's needs is one of the greatest challenges facing Solidarity. On all past experience the length of time for which workers will suppress economic demands more directly related to the specific demands of their industry is limited. Since August 1980, powerful groups of workers have used their industrial muscle for general, not specifically industrial, purposes. Solidarity itself will have difficulties coping with all the economic pressures from their 8 – 10 million members spread amongst many different industries and occupations. Neither the union, nor the Polish government, as it looked over its shoulder and wondered what the implications of fundamental economic reform meant for other communist economies, has had, or will have, an easy task.

Chapter 9

Render unto Caesar . . . . . . Solidarity and the Church

Snow fell and the temperature was minus 20 degrees centigrade as the crowds gathered for Mass at four o'clock in the afternoon in Walbrzych's main church one Thursday in December 1980. Walbrzych is one of the coal-rich areas of Silesia. The rugged hilly terrain is not unlike South Wales, though the Walbrzych miners boast that difficult as their coal is to extract from the awkward seams, it is the highest quality coking anthracite and coking coal to be found anywhere in the world. Now on 4th December 1980, they had taken the day off and were coming to Mass. December 4th is St Barbara's day, and St Barbara is the patron saint of Polish miners. Just as the early Christian Church absorbed pagan feasts and turned them into religious festivals like Christmas, so the post-war rulers of Poland took a religious day like December 4th, St Barbara's day, and made it an official miners' holiday when festivals and feasts were laid on by the old official miners' union. Regional or even national figures would come to Silesia to award labour medals and make speeches about the need for greater productivity in the pits.

The creation of Solidarity meant that for the first time since the war the miners of Walbrzych were able to celebrate their patron saint's day in a traditional religious fashion. The high ceilinged red-brick church was crammed with miners, their families and the local townspeople. Outside, in the freezing cold, the local miners' chairman chatted with Jan Litynski, a KOR member and an editor of *Robotnik,* who had been in Walbrzych advising the miners since they broke away from the old union and set up a regional Solidarity organisation in September 1980. Inside, High Mass was being said by the Archbishop of Wroclaw, who preached a sermon invoking the Polish struggle for independence against the Russians in the 19th century. He recalled the steadfast "solidarity" of St Barbara, who died rather than forswear her faith. He gave thanks to present-day Solidarity and urged parents to teach their children the Polish traditions. The Mass finished on a light-hearted note as a miner, dressed in the traditional black costume of Silesia,chatted on the altar with the Archbishop and even exchanged his hat with its large white feathers for the Archbishop's mitre. As the packed church sang the great and (even to atheistic ears) moving, Polish hymn,

Boze cos Polske (God who has protected Poland) — perhaps the only other hymn that touches *Boze cos Polske* for national-religious intensity is to hear *Faith of Our Fathers* sung by Irish Catholics in Ulster — a procession of miners dressed in their black costumes wound its way through the church. Each pit was represented with its flag. On the flag of the Maurice Thorez (the former French Communist Party leader) pit there was firmly pinned a large Solidarity badge. On the breasts of the miners, intermingled with war or labour productivity medals, were little red and white Solidarity badges. Each group of miners carried a small statue of St Barbara which had been blessed by the Archbishop, and would be placed in each pit. As the procession, with flags held high, wound its way into the streets of Walbrzych, people's eyes were wet, as different emotions — religious, nationalist, and defiance for those who had prevented the celebration of St Barbara's day as a religious feast during the past 30 years — could be seen almost visibly surging through the minds of the thousands of Poles present.

The Church and Solidarity

From the very beginning of the Gdansk strike, the imagery of the Church was everywhere. On the railings of the Lenin Shipyard workers hung big colour photographs of Pope John Paul II. Walesa always had a badge with the picture of the Black Virgin of Czestochowa pinned on his lapel. High on the list of twenty-one demands was that the Church should be allowed to broadcast Mass on State radio. The conference hall where the Inter-Factory Strike Committee met had a crucifix behind the platform. Three days into the strike, when workers were hesitant about staying on to occupy the shipyard, once the initial demands over more money and Anna Walentynowicz's reinstatement had been met, the strike organisers persuaded a Gdansk priest to come and say Sunday Mass (against his Bishop's wishes) to the occupying shipyard workers and so stop them from drifting home.

Since the strike, the Church's, at least symbolic, presence is everywhere. No Solidarity office is complete without a crucifix and portraits of Pope John Paul II. Major Solidarity public ceremonies, like the unveiling of the monuments to the workers killed in 1970, or Solidarity's May 3rd celebrations, have religious services woven into them. Western magazines seem to have published as many pictures of Walesa on his knees in church as they have of him addressing workers. Editorial writers in many Western papers have talked of Solidarity almost as if it were under the Church's control. Yet at the same time Solidarity can publish an official document about itself which is intended for distribution to trade unions outside Poland which categorically states that the union "identifies itself with no ideology and no religion. It is true that among the union symbols those of the Catholic religion are of great consequence. This reflects the respect which society, most of the people being Catholic, has for the moral authority of the Church. But the union itself, as a social movement, is secular. It acknowledges the Christian values to be the foundation of European culture, but it is not politically related to the Church, nor does it consider the Catholic social doctrine to be its programme".

The worldwide importance of what has been happening inside Poland since August 1980 is because it constitutes a major victory for the working class. The fact that Polish workers are all baptised, and for the most part practising Catholics, and that Solidarity's ceremonial involvement with the Church is so obvious should not blind one to the fact that Solidarity operates quite independently of the Church. That is not to say that Solidarity's national and regional leaders do not meet with cardinals, archbishops, bishops and priests, and listen to what they have to say with a greater degree of moral respect than when they have to listen to lay intellectuals. One should not confuse paying spiritual leaders moral respect with taking orders from them. Priests do not attend National Co-ordinating Commissions, though Cardinal Wyszynski's senior lay adviser, Professor Kukulowicz, attended some National Co-ordinating Commission sessions; nor are bishops members of regional praesidiums. There is not a single recorded incident in which the intervention of a Church leader has made any critical difference to a Solidarity decision. The Church's caution first manifested itself during the Gdansk strike and has continued ever since. But this moderation fully corresponds to the political analysis of some Solidarity leaders who need no urging from the Church to stop certain types of strike, or to curtail more provocative demands from the base. It is not necessary to be a Catholic to be a moderate, nor do decisions to call off general strikes (such as the one threatened over the Bydgoszcz incident) reflect undue Church influence, so much as majority decisions taken after long debate by Solidarity's leadership, which is quite capable of making up its own mind, based on the available evidence.

Keeping Alive Poland's National Spirit

Yet at the same time there is convincing evidence for arguing that without the Church, and, in particular, without the example set by the Church in how to resist incorporation by a one-party State, Solidarity could not have come into existence. The historical importance of the Church in keeping the Polish culture and national identity alive during the long years when Poland was divided and ruled by the great empires of Central Europe — Russia, Germany and Austria-Hungary — is undeniable. As in Ireland under British rule, the Church offered a spiritual national identity that provided solace to a people whose political self-expression was denied by the foreign occupier. It is no accident that Ireland and Poland are Europe's most intensely practising Catholic countries with no substantial anti-clerical politics that developed in other Catholic countries like France and Spain, where the Church was long seen as part of the governing establishment, rather than the champion of national self-identity. For thirty years the primate of Poland, Cardinal Stefan Wyszynski, represented for many Poles the enduring symbol of their country's difference, and its refusal to be subjected to Soviet hegemony. The 250,000 Poles who turned out for his funeral in Warsaw indicate the support he had. The Communist rulers of Poland provided the Catholics with something approaching the figure of a martyr through their early persecution and imprisonment of Wyszynski. There are now three times as many priests as in pre-war Poland. If you drive through many of Poland's poorest villages you will see a well-built church in the midst of the rural poverty. Yet the Polish Church cannot occupy itself with two of the main social concerns of the Catholic Church in the non-communist world — the control of female fertility and children's education. Birth control and abortion more or less on demand are generally available in Poland and, whatever the Church's teaching, they are freely taken up. The State has complete control of education from the kindergarten upwards, though the Church runs religious classes outside school. The Polish Church found itself deprived, therefore, of its traditional role as the guardian of personal sexual relations and was unable to form the young minds at school. Unlike the pre-war Polish Church, which, in order to safeguard its land and properties, was deeply enmeshed with the anti working-class ruling establishment, Cardinal Wyszynski's Church became a champion of human rights and freedom of expression, and in that way firmly established its credentials as being separate and apart from the ruling organs of the State. The Church publicly sympathised with the Jews persecuted in the anti-semitic purges of 1968 and expressed support for the "rightful struggle of the Polish workers" during the strikes of 1970 and again in 1976. It did not formally support KOR and the other oppositionists in the period 1976 – 80, but Church leaders always criticised attempts by the security police and authorities to harass or arrest dissident intellectuals.

Within a Church which had to be tolerated, if not fully accepted by the State, there was also room for widening the boundaries of intellectual freedom. The Clubs of the Catholic Intelligentsia in

Warsaw, Cracow, Wroclaw, Poznan and Torun, provided, not just meeting places, but opportunities for non-communist intellectuals from different disciplines to meet, exchange ideas and forge links. The Catholic intellectual journals, although limited in circulation because of restrictions on paper availability, also showed the possibility of maintaining systems of thought and expression that was independent of the State ideology. Again, it is important to stress that although the word 'Catholic' figures in the title of these clubs and journals, they were not necessarily theologically or spiritually orientated. Although religious subjects featured as discussion topics, questions of economics, politics, history, culture, were endlessly debated. This parallel intellectual life was relatively open and tolerated. It should not be confused with the samzidat publications of dissident circles in the Soviet Union, or the discussion groups inside Czechoslovakia. The tacit concordat between the State and the Polish Church created a space, not just for Catholics, but also for lay intellectuals who discussed secular subjects. This developed, not only a taste for, but also the practical experience of, organising discussion groups or editorial boards that were clearly separate from, and independent of, Party and State. After the creation of Solidarity many of these intellectuals turned to the new union to offer advice and help. Long before August 1980, in the big university towns, there already existed an experienced cadre of intellectuals associated with the Catholic Church who had the experience and the confidence to know that forms of organisation and expression independent of the State and Party were perfectly possible. One cannot start a mass social movement like Solidarity from scratch. The Catholic Church in Poland had provided an example of an independent force co-existing with the one-party State. It had also helped nurture the growth of thousands of independent lay people who would help Solidarity firmly implant its roots.

The Polish Pope

Never before in its history has Poland had two such internationally renowned sons as Lech Walesa and Pope John Paul II. The election in 1978 of Cracow's Cardinal Karol Wojtyla to be Pope John Paul II seemed to express international endorsement of the role and activities of the Polish Church. The new Pope's dynamic, public-relations conscious style carried the papacy to a position of world authority that it had not enjoyed for a long time. When he visited Poland in June 1979, more than half-a-million people flocked to Southern Poland to greet him. The entire logistical organisation of this mass movement of people was carried out by the Church, helped by State or regional authorities. Neither police nor militia were to be seen. It was an important psychological first in Eastern Europe. For the first time there took place what was, in effect, a mass (large numbers of people, not the religious service) meeting which was perfectly organised, calm and purposeful, and yet, had nothing to do with the Communist Party. Bringing people together for mass events is an important part of the development of a popular movement. The sense one has of being united with scores of thousands of like-minded people, and of feeling far less vulnerable to being individually targetted by authority gives one a confidence-strengthening belief in one's ability to defy those in power. One should not romanticise the event, but some Solidarity activists talk of the Pope's visit as the point when, for the first time, Poles saw and felt their own strength as a mass force.

The presence of a Polish Pope in the Vatican has added a different kind of safeguard for Solidarity. Stalin's sneering question: "How many divisions does the Pope have?" seems even more irrelevant today than when he posed it during the war. At the height of one of the Soviet invasion scares a rumour went round Warsaw that should Russian troops cross the border, the Pope was going to smuggle himself back into Poland to be with his people. An unlikely story, yet both the Polish and Soviet leaderships cannot but take into consideration the international influence of the Pope, especially in strongly Catholic third world countries where Moscoworientated Communist Parties or where communist-led national liberation movements are struggling to win popular support. For Polish workers themselves, whose lives since infancy have been surrounded by religious symbolism, the fact of having a fellow countryman sitting in St. Peter's must seem little short of miraculous and a sign from heaven, as it were, that Poland, at least for the time being, has favoured nation status with God.

According to Edmund Baluka the Poles are "great hypocrites" about their Church. It is perhaps too easy to be overly impressed by the outward religiosity of the Poles, the crucifixes and pictures of the Pope. It does not follow that the Church has substantial influence, let alone exercises power, over Solidarity. The undoubted commitment to the Catholic faith of the Polish workers does not tell us what political, economic and social decisions they will take. To go to Mass every Sunday, as do most Solidarity members, is no guide as to how they vote in a democratic decision-making process. In 1981 the Pope campaigned and spoke out against Italy's abortion law. Despite the wave of highly emotional sympathy that he enjoyed following the attempt on his life, the Italian — Catholic — population decisively rejected his advice and, in a referendum, voted to endorse the State provision of abortion.

On the day after Cardinal Wyszynski died, three members of a

Solidarity delegation who were in the United States appeared on the MacNeil-Lehrer Report, a prestigious networked television current affairs programme. For the first ten minutes the two American interviewers bombarded them with questions about what the death of Wyszynski would mean for Poland and for Solidarity. The Polish workers' answers conveyed a deep sense of the tremendous moral respect that they had for the late Cardinal, but none of them could think of a single change in the activities of Solidarity that would be brought about by the Cardinal's death. The American interviewers were clearly disappointed, but like many other Western media commentators, they had made the false connection between, on the one hand, the position of the Church in Polish society, and the religious beliefs of individual Poles; and, on the other hand, the idea that the Church therefore plays an instrumental role in guiding Solidarity.

It may be that there are some within the Polish Church who would like to have more influence over Solidarity. Like all powerful institutions, the Polish Church is a highly political body. Unfortunately, unlike Solidarity, the Church's leaders do not debate their differences in public, or make the minutes of the Bishops' Conference available for public distribution. There is clearly some resentment in some Church sections at the role of certain Solidarity activists who stress the secular and socialist ambitions of the new union. In December 1980, Father Alojzy Orszulik, Director of the Press Office of the Polish Episcopate, issued a statement critical of KOR and Jacek Kuron. It implied that the continuing presence of KOR activists was unwelcome to the Church and even hinted that the Church would not react if the authorities took action against Kuron. Orszulik's statement was widely criticised in Poland by many priests and Catholic lay intellectuals, and the Church has not made such explicitly condemnatory remarks about the secular, socialist wing in Solidarity since. Even Cardinal Wyszynski kept his distance from Orszulik's remarks by receiving KOR member, Adam Michnik, shortly after the statement. It is reasonable to suppose that the physical weakness and illness of Cardinal Wyszynski during the last year of his life suspended what would otherwise have been a political fight within the Church on how to deal with Solidarity. Now that a figure of such authority inside the Church is no longer there, different factions will probably more openly begin vying for influence.

According to Adam Michnik, the KOR activist and lecturer at the flying university, the Polish Church offers, from a long-term perspective, a perfect model for the co-existence of an independent social formation and those who hold power. "This model unites two fundamental factors: an understanding of realities; and constant pressure on those in power." But Michnik added that there were different tendencies in the Church: there were those who saw the possibilities of an "Iranisation" of Poland with a weakening central power confronted by religious forces thinking only of its overthrow; those who wanted the Church to come to a deal with the State in exchange for increased ecclesiastical liberties; and then finally, priests close to Solidarity who wanted an open Church in a pluralist society — "a Church that does not want to be authoritarian, but which defends its own rights as part of the general defence of human rights". In Michnik's view, the Pope belongs to this latter category. When he made this analysis in November 1980, Michnik stressed that there was more than one tendency at work within the episcopate.

Although I have tried to show that it is wrong to inflate the Church's role in Solidarity or to assume the hidden hand of the Bishops on the occasions when Solidarity draws back from confrontation, it is equally mistaken to dismiss the Church, as do some Western left-wingers, as an irrelevant, backward-looking force that Solidarity will jettison as the Polish workers grow stronger. The future of both institutions is bound together. Solidarity, its members and the large sections of the Polish population who are not members of, but who support, Solidarity, draw confidence from the Church's support for the new union. The Church, in turn, knows that only the workers have enough power to force through real political changes that can open up society in the direction that the Church has always claimed it wanted to go. The Church in Poland has enjoyed its greatest ascendancy under a period of "Godless" communist rule. Since the arrival of Solidarity, however, the Church has lost its role of being the sole independent champion of the Polish people. The Church's search for a new, and from its point of view, satisfactory, role, will be an important element in the changes Poland is living through.

Chapter 10

All the News
that's Fit to Print

Leszek Dlouchy looked up from his typewriter. The editor of one of the two Solidarity newspapers officially printed on State printing presses, was having difficulty in composing the front page lead for that week's edition. Until the Autumn of 1980, he had never had to use a typewriter or compose a news story. Neither has much to do with his former job as a mechanic in a Szczecin shipyard. Now he heads a team which each week brings out *Jednosc* (Unity), which sells 100,000 copies in North West Poland. *Jednosc* was launched in January 1981, followed four months later by *Tygodnik Solidarnosc* (Weekly Solidarity), Solidarity's official national newspaper, whose 500,000 copies are the most sought-after newspapers anywhere in the world. The two newspapers are the top of a pyramid of daily bulletins, weekly and monthly plant and regional journals, radio cassette recordings, posters and leaflets, which form Solidarity's information network. Since August 1980 considerable effort has been put into extending and improving Solidarity's communications with its members and society in general. "An end to censorship" remains one of the ambitions that Solidarity's leaders most often mention when asked what changes they would like to see introduced.

Control of the mass media is one of the essential components of communist rule in Eastern Europe. One does not have to be a champion of the press in capitalist countries, with its obsessive sensationalism and deep-rooted bias against working-class organisations and their causes, to note that the media in one-party States allow no criticism of the State's rulers and offer no outlet for workers' protests. The media under both communist and capitalist ideological systems defend the *status quo,* the difference ironically being that in the West, where the media permit dissenting voices and are supplemented by the publication of fringe labour movement journals, thereby providing a superficial impression of openness and plurality, they are nevertheless, much more successful in transmitting the complex set of economic, social, political and cultural values associated with capital (which, after all, in most cases formally owns the media) than the media in communist countries, which through an unvaried and unchallenged peddling of the

Party line succeed in convincing the readership that both the media and the political message they convey are not to be trusted.

The Search for Free Media

The emphasis that Solidarity places on the need for media freedoms is underlined in the Gdansk Agreement. The first and second points, which deal with the right to form independent trade unions and the right to strike are followed by point number three: "To respect freedom of expression and publication as upheld by the Constitution of People's Poland, and to take no measures against independent publications, as well as to grant access to the mass media to representatives of all religions". At the earliest stage, therefore, the striking workers were putting forward a claim for media freedom and giving it a higher priority than economic demands. Getting a few thousand extra zlotys or reinstatement for victimised workers would turn out to be a hollow victory unless there were independent trade unions, a right to strike and independent newspapers to guarantee the other advances.

One of the first acts of the striking workers in Gdansk was to start a daily news bulletin which someone decided to call *Solidarity*. It was from that simple, duplicated news-sheet that the union was to take its name. The model was that of *Robotnik,* consisting of extremely closely typed articles, run off on Roneo-type duplicating machines. The world's television screens witnessed the popularity of those early issues of the strikers' bulletin as crowds of people fought to get hold of a copy flung over the railings of the Lenin Shipyard. In fact, issue No. 1 of the *Solidarity* strike bulletin, dated 23rd August 1980, contained an appeal for accurate information in the official press: "The whole country awaits genuine and accurate news from the strike-bound Baltic coast. But the news in the press, radio and television is both distorted and incomplete. The existence of the Inter-Factory Strike Committees in Gdansk, Szczecin and Elblag is ignored. Nothing has been said about the fact that the strike action is co-ordinated and directed by the democratically elected Inter-Factory Strike Committees."

Many trade union and KOR activists, and certainly all the political leadership in Poland, used to listen regularly to the broadcasts of Radio Free Europe, the American financed radio station that broadcasts to Eastern Europe from Munich. The Soviet Union has exerted tremendous pressure on the West German government to close down Radio Free Europe, charging that its transmissions are a leftover from the height of the Cold War. Few commentators doubt that the reason for Radio Free Europe's existence is ideological rather than disinterestedly journalistic. The fact remains that to many people in Eastern Europe it is the only source of information about workers' struggles and dissidents' movements in their own countries. During the strikes preceding the Gdansk strike, Radio Free Europe would broadcast details of who had gone on strike and where, only a few hours after the strikes had begun. With a complete blackout of news in the Polish media, the Polish workers could not be blamed for tuning in to foreign stations such as the BBC or Radio Free Europe to find out what was happening. The Soviet Union and other East European States could close down Radio Free Europe overnight by the simple expedient of allowing their journalists to try and report the truth.

Instead of waiting for the Government to provide access to the State printed newspapers, Solidarity has developed what is effectively an alternative press based on regional and plant bulletins. The quality and quantity of this unofficial press has grown stronger with Solidarity's continued existence. Unlike many strike or campaign bulletins, which wither away once the heat of the confrontation has cooled down, the Solidarity press keeps improving. In appearance, the various news-sheets are not very inviting. Pages are crowded with tiny, hard to read, text. The printing, whether lithographic or duplicated, is usually of poor quality, with plates and stencils used well past the stage where they would normally be thrown away. The readership couldn't care less about the technical quality. For the first time, in more than a generation, they are getting news and comment written and published in Poland that can be completely trusted. The only limitation on the Solidarity bulletins is the availability of paper and printing equipment. Most regions have weekly print runs of 20,000 copies of between six and twelve pages. Big regions like Cracow and Wroclaw turn out up to 100,000 copies weekly. Many of the large plants also produce bulletins with large print runs. In Warsaw, Solidarity produces two daily bulletins, and queues of messengers form to take it away to factories and Solidarity centres in the districts around Warsaw.

These bulletins are produced by small teams of workers and, often, students from local universities and polytechnics. To begin with, those who had been active in KOR and in the production and distribution of *Robotnik* provided the core of the Solidarity journal editors. *Robotnik* continues to appear. Printed in six regional centres, it now has a print run of 250,000. But as the new union sank and spread its roots deeper and wider, people who had never written an article or laid out a page, began to take over.

What Solidarity Writes About

The contents of the plant and regional bulletins is a mixture of general articles, statements from national Solidarity, and reports of what is happening in other parts of Poland. The 21st November

1980 issue of the Wroclaw regional Solidarity bulletin led with an editorial written by an intellectual on the importance of plant election. The basic purpose of Solidarity, he wrote, was to create democratic freedoms. Solidarity was committed to truth which would be its contribution to governing the country. The worst danger was that the union would be taken over by careerists and opportunists. Solidarity's main concerns are the problems faced by workers in the plants. The writer went on to defend the regional structure of Solidarity and touched upon the question of self-management. The next piece was a report of the Independence Day (November 11th) celebrations in Gdansk, followed by a lengthy analysis of the moral and political role of the union.

Solidarity bulletins often carry articles on Polish history. For example, the front page of the Cracow Solidarity Bulletin of November 22nd reproduced a report of the 1830 uprising against the Russians. This was followed by an article on how to go about plant elections, an extract from a speech at a teachers' meeting, a list of the demands raised by secondary school teachers, an article on environment protection, an article on current economic-political problems, two letters to the editor and a statement from the Warsaw region of Solidarity about the arrest of the printers in connection with the secret Prosecutor General's document on harassing Solidarity and KOR members.

The 12-page issue of the weekly Bydgoszcz regional Solidarity magazine of 30th April 1981 was still dominated by articles connected with the Bydgoszcz incident and the agreement reached between the union and the authorities following the incident. Separate articles analysed the agreement; a lawyer wrote a piece about its legal validity; and there was a page of verbatim extracts from the speeches made at the signing session. Then followed one article on the celebrations planned for May 3rd and a piece on the importance of the 1791 constitution. Two articles dealt with subjects of direct interest to workers: one explained how to resist attempts by management to dismiss workers, while the second strongly criticised the system of choosing which schoolchildren go on to higher education. According to the writer, it is strongly biased against workers' children. There was a long interview with Stefan Kurowski, one of Solidarity's experts, about his work on the economic reform package being discussed with the government. Finally, there was an article called Poetry and Politics, which discussed the work of the Polish poet, Antoni Pawlak.

Tygodnik Solidarnosc and Jednosc

The two main titles of Solidarity's press are *Tygodnik Solidarnosc* (Weekly Solidarity) and *Jednosc* (Unity). Both are tabloid-sized papers consisting of between eight and sixteen pages. They are professionally printed in State printing houses. Being printed by the State means that both papers have to be submitted to the State office for censorship. The government resisted for many months before it allowed the publication of *Tygodnik Solidarnosc*. Its first issue did not appear until 3rd April 1981. Apart from problems with the State, there was a considerable dispute inside Solidarity about what kind of paper it should be, and who should edit it. The question of the editor would settle the style of the paper. The favoured candidate was Tadeuz Mazowiecki, who was editor of the radical Catholic journal *Wiez* (Link). Mazowiecki had driven to Gdansk soon after the Lenin Shipyard strike and, together with Professor Bronislaw Geremek had headed the Committee of experts who had helped the workers during the strike, and ever since. Transferring Western political categories to Polish political relationships is a risky business, but most commentators would place Mazowiecki on the more cautious, Church-orientated wing of Solidarity. Certainly, he had the support of the Church to be the editor of the national Solidarity paper. The left KOR-orientated wing of Solidarity felt a little miffed at the proposal of Mazowiecki as the new paper's editor as they considered, with some justification, that both their experience and their pre-August 1980 commitment to workers' journalism through the publication of *Robotnik* entitled them to a major role in what was, after all, to be the first totally independent national workers' publication in Eastern Europe. In the end, those close to KOR could not decide on a single candidate and the person they would have liked to push forward as editor, Karol Modzelewski, declined to stand against Mazowiecki. Journalists who had worked on *Robotnik* also refused to work for Mazowiecki. One of them explained: "It was not that we were against him, but we felt Solidarity should not, as it were, put all its eggs in one journalistic basket. We wanted to keep producing *Robotnik,* help with the regional and plant bulletins, and develop other forms of communicating with the members. Solidarity has to have a real internal plurality of information". The first few issues of *Tygodnik Solidarnosc* were fairly cautious. The former Szczecin activist Edmund Baluka told me that when reading the articles he could feel the censor's presence in the pages, while the *Financial Times* correspondent in Warsaw, Chris Bobinski, said that Mazowiecki had succeeded in producing an independent paper that would not provoke heart seizures when read in the Russian embassy in Warsaw. In fact, even radical Solidarity activists acknowledge that *Tygodnik Solidarnosc* is doing a necessary and good job in widening the scope of the union's publications and helping to establish Solidarity as a routine feature of Polish society. An extremely radical journal that provoked constant confrontation with the authorities would open up a new and unwanted field of government/Solidarity conflict.

The government permits 500,000 copies of *Tygodnik Solidarnosc* to be printed each week. It is impossible to buy one in a news kiosk. The paper's print run is divided up for Solidarity's different regions and they, in turn, parcel it out to the major factories, or sell it to local Solidarity activitists. A factory with 10,000 employees would get twenty-five copies, which are placed in the factory library. If paper and government permission were available, it could easily sell several million copies.

Jednosc, which sells 100,000 copies in the three voivodships around Szczecin, is regarded as *Tygodnik Solidarnosc's* more radical little sister. *Jednosc* began life as a single-side news-sheet produced by Solidarity activists in Szczecin. It was separate from the regional Solidarity bulletin and was produced by a small team under Leszek Dlouchy, a Warski shipyard mechanic still only in his mid-twenties.

At the end of 1980 Dlouchy decided to go beyond a news-sheet produced on the limited printing equipment possessed by Szczecin Solidarity. Thanks to the relatively good relations between the moderate Szczecin Solidarity leadership and the regional authorities Dlouchy was allowed to use a State-owned printing press to re-launch *Jednosc* as a professionally produced, professionally designed newspaper. Its 100,000 copies are distributed only in the area around Szczecin. 35,000 copies go out through the numerous news kiosks, and you have to be up early to find one. 65,000 copies are sold in workplaces and Solidarity offices in the towns inside the region. Dlouchy explained the difficult early days of the paper: "At the beginning we had big problems with the official censorship. They stopped several articles from appearing. So we organised a strike in the printing house and stopped official publications from appearing. They got the message and stopped being so heavy-handed. They still look at the paper and I suppose there is a process of self-censorship, which means we cannot publish everything that we would like".

According to the Poles themselves *Jednosc* is considered healthily iconoclastic and it is not afraid to tackle some of Solidarity's internal divisions and personality differences. Dlouchy himself is a member of the regional praesidium, thus providing a link between the Solidarity leadership and the paper. But the link is tenuous and *Jednosc* is not seen as the official mouthpiece of Solidarity in the region. There is a full-time editorial team of seven people, none of whom come from a journalistic background. Said Dlouchy: "We started off as amateurs and we are learning on the job. We are not professional journalists and therefore we do not have the ideological luggage of years of working for communist papers to unload".

Apart from *Jednosc* and *Tygodnik Solidarnosc*, Solidarity had not been successful in talks with the authorities for permission to produce more newspapers and journals on the State printing presses. In many cases they would not be granted access, but Solidarity is also reluctant to enmesh itself too closely with the State censorship, or become too dependent on the State for printing purposes. In 1944, at the height of the Nazi occupation of Poland, there were 211 separate privately-owned printing firms in Wroclaw. Now there are only 8, all owned by the State. Solidarity is more keen to develop its own printing operation. Three small, but completely equipped printing operations were being set up in the Summer of 1981 with equipment paid for by trade unions outside Poland. A team of Solidarity printers had also been in Sweden on a training course organised by the Swedish printworkers' union.

This reliance on self-help makes political sense. The experience after 1956 and 1970 suggests that for workers to rely on the authorities to keep their word in Poland without developing their own independent means of organisation and communication is a fatal error. But Solidarity's own printing operation is so stretched that it can barely keep up with the demand for duplicated or simple offset produced material. Solidarity has yet to develop a system for publishing longer pamphlets and books that can provide organisational and political training for its activists. Before 1980 the unofficial publishing house *Nowa,* headed by Miroslaw Chojecki, produced more than 150 titles, including the poems of Czeslaw Milosz, the Nobel prize-winning Polish poet, who, because he lived in exile, was not published officially in Poland until he won the Nobel Prize in 1980. The people who produced books for *Nowa* overlapped with KOR, and free trade union activists, and were generally placed in the same oppositionist category, but the publishing policy of *Nowa* was orientated to cultural and historical topics, and publishing translations of forbidden foreign authors, such as George Orwell, Gunter Grass and Osip Mandelstam. Few, if any, of *Nowa's* books were directly connected to workers' problems. It should be stressed that Poland has hundreds of books about its working class which have been published by official publishing houses. None of them dealt with recent history as experienced by Polish workers, nor did officially approved books concern themselves with current problems faced by Polish workers, such as health and safety. Since August 1980 *Nowa* has been less active in publishing full-length books, mainly because what oppositionist energy and black market supplies there are in Poland have gone into producing Solidarity bulletins and news-sheets. The problem of publishing longer pamphlets and books in Poland in order to build the new union is one that has yet to be fully solved. *Nowa* now works closely with Solidarity and has set up a network of 200 lending libraries with books and periodicals published outside the censorship system. The libraries are established on request from a Solidarity branch in large enterprises.

AS, Solidarity's News Agency

An extremely important link in Solidarity's information network is the Warsaw-based Solidarity news agency, AS, edited by Helena Luczywo, a former KOR activist and *Robotnik* editor, and a part-time Warsaw correspondent for the London *Daily Telegraph* (she left the *Daily Telegraph,* despite the protection that being one of its correspondents provided, because she could no longer stomach the paper's simplistic anti-Socialism that accompanied all its coverage of the events surrounding the development of Solidarity). The Solidarity news agency bulletin is now one of the most important elements in the union's information system. Each week a small team of people driven along by Helen Luczywo's friendly but unrelenting energy, work late into the night inside the Solidarity headquarters producing a thick, stapled volume of news reports of what is being done and said by Solidarity, or done to Solidarity by the police, Party or government authorities. Pages are typed and then reduced photographically so as to fit three or four normal sized pages on to a single page of the AS (Solidarity Agency) bulletin. This means that the AS bulletin sometimes carries the equivalent of 200 pages of news and information. The AS bulletin was launched in February 1981. It is divided into five sections. The first carries verbatim extracts from the debates at the National Co-ordinating Commission. The passion for openness and for the right of ordinary members to read what is being said by their representatives is one of the hallmarks of Solidarity. However, the proceedings of the national Praesidium are discreetly edited by the AS team. At some stage all trade unions have to discuss tactics against employers or their own internal divisions. Publication of such debates would provide considerable help to a union's opponents. The problem is to find the balance between what necessarily should be kept confidential, without drifting into a situation in which rank and file members feel that major decisions inside the union or important negotiations with employers all take place behind closed doors, and in a manner which effectively excludes the membership from knowing what is being said in its name.

The second section of the AS bulletin carries news from the regions. This is compiled from telex reports that the regions send into Warsaw. According to Helena Luczywo, it is the weakest section of the AS bulletin, "because people do not go into enough detail". This is followed by all the full texts of official resolutions and statements published by Solidarity. The fourth section carries articles by Solidarity's experts on discussions, new ideas or negotiations in the various fields in which Solidarity is trying to evolve policy. Finally, and this section can often amount to half of the AS bulletin, there are reprinted Solidarity plant and regional bulletins from all over the country. Obviously, each single local bulletin cannot be carried each week, but over a month-long period the reader of the AS bulletin would have the most detailed knowledge of what Solidarity was doing, saying and thinking, not just in the cities, but all over Poland.

Only 1,500 copies of the AS bulletin are produced and are sold at the relatively high price of 50 zlotys (65p or $1.50). Copies are sent to all the Solidarity regional offices. The AS bulletin has very quickly become part of the glue that binds Solidarity together throughout Poland.

The Warsaw regional office of Solidarity also provides a tape cassette service. Produced by Marek Chlebowicz, who has a job with the Polish State radio, the tapes are properly produced programmes. Chlebowicz was in Bydgoszcz in March 1981, when the militia beat up local Solidarity leaders badly, thus provoking one of the worst crises in Solidarity's history. The cassette he made of the incident was broadcast on factory radio systems and inside Solidarity offices all over Poland and helped to counter government propaganda which portrayed the Bydgoszcz incident as the work of irresponsible elements in Solidarity.

Workers' Radio

In most countries, plant radio systems are important tools for management control, either by playing soothing music to while away the tedium of assembly-line work, or for making management announcements. Some unknown genius in the Gdansk strike suggested that the negotiations with the government ministers should be broadcast on the Lenin Shipyard radio system to the delegates from other factories and to the strikers in the yard. This has been widely copied in other big plants, and the loudspeakers originally installed as a means of controlling the workforce are now used to keep workers alert and informed about their new status. As well as cassette recordings, such as those produced by Chlebowicz, there is a constant flow of recordings of Solidarity's meetings or speeches. If you attend a big Solidarity meeting, you see very few notebooks; instead there are dozens of cassette recorders held up to catch what is being said. In some plants, Huta Warszawa (Warsaw's steel plant), for example, negotiations between Solidarity representatives and the plant management are broadcast live over the loudspeaker system.

Poland is the poster capital of the world. Each year since the war Polish graphic artists have carried off the world's top prizes for posters. Since August 1980, much of that talent has been made available for Solidarity. Many striking and brilliantly designed posters have been produced for the new union. They are to be found all over Poland, mostly inside factories, offices and schools. Solidarity has adopted a policy of not plastering the streets with its posters, so as to avoid small-scale friction with the authorities. Together with the union badges, which are seen everywhere, and many well-designed leaflets, the quality and quantity of Solidarity posters is a public indication of the strength and resources of the new union. It is a way for Solidarity to announce that it is here to stay.

Solidarity handles its external relations with journalists with a panache from which the public relations officers of many Western organisations could learn much. Their basic policy is one of openness and availability. Well before the August strike in Gdansk the KOR activists realised the importance of telling Western journalists about the wave of strikes being unleashed in protest against the food price rises. In late July and August 1980 Jacek Kuron's flat in Warsaw became an information centre used by Western journalists needing information about the strikes. Although secondary to the work of informing Poles (7 million leaflets were produced in July and August 1980) the briefing of Western journalists was very important in order to internationalise the workers' action. As soon as the importance of the Gdansk strike was realised, Western journalists poured into the Baltic coast region. They found workers ready to talk, and this policy has been maintained ever since.

Lech Walesa must by now be the most interviewed trade unionist in the world. In Gdansk, Solidarity set up an Information and Press Bureau to brief visiting journalists, arrange interviews with the national leadership and fix up factory visits. It also publishes a regular bulletin. In Warsaw, press relations are handled by Janusz Onyszkiewicz, a mathematics lecturer at Warsaw University, whose three years' post-graduate work at Leeds University had given him near perfect English, with even a slight Yorkshire accent. In March 1981 Onyszkiewicz replaced Karol Modzelewski as Solidarity's national press spokesperson and he is often seen on Polish television issuing statements on Solidarity's behalf.

In his office in Warsaw is a team of young graduates from the excellent language departments of Warsaw University, who organise

Solidarity's weekly press conference, brief reporters and act as in-
terpreters for visiting journalists.

The Official Media

Solidarity has had a long fight to get access to the official media.
Polish newspaper readers or television viewers say that there has
been a great opening up of the Polish media in general since August
1980. The Polish Journalists' Union rid itself of its Party-
appointed chairman and elected a noted liberal journalist, Stefan
Bratkowski, in his place. Bratkowski is a Party member and has
good access to the Polish leadership, especially the reformist wing.
The opening up of the Polish media has been slow and cautious,
avoiding revolutionary changes that would overly provoke Soviet
concern. In some regional newspapers, Solidarity has its own col-
umn, or at least, its statements are impartially presented. Poland's
political weekly, *Polityka,* edited by the reformist Mieczyslaw
Rakowski, who was made a deputy premier in February 1981 as a
major gesture to Party reformers, has carried long and politically
challenging interviews with Solidarity leaders. The national daily
Zycie Warszawy (Life of Warsaw) has carried a considerable
number of articles about Solidarity. It devoted almost an entire
page to an accurate and impartial account of Edmund Baluka's re-
entry into Poland and how his arrival was handled by workers and
the regional Solidarity office in Szczecin. It would be difficult to
imagine a newspaper in Great Britain or the United States that
would ever report a major trade union story with such
scrupulousness.

On 16th May 1981 Solidarity came to an agreement with the
government permitting the union to broadcast its own programmes
on State television and radio. The union would be able to appear
once a month, broadcasting its views on "important socio-
economic issues". It would have 0.2 per cent of the total air time on
radio and 0.8 per cent on television. It seemed a major
breakthrough, unprecedented certainly, in Western countries,
where formal trade union control of even the smallest portion of
television or radio air time would be bitterly resisted by both State
and private broadcasting stations. But the official announcement
added an ominous rider that all programmes would be subject to
State censorship. On the same day as that the government offered
Solidarity air time, the all-powerful Communist Party Politburo
confirmed Stefan Olszowski, one of the most hardline anti-
Solidarity Party leaders as the man responsible for the mass media,
despite widespread criticism by Party members of his handling of
information policy. Nor, despite its seeming generosity, had the
government moved any further in promoting a complete liberalisa-

tion of the censorship laws, as promised in the Gdansk Agreement.

The demand for an "end to censorship" remains, therefore, an important and continuing objective for Solidarity. Solidarity's formal demands are for censorship to be limited to matters of State security and for an independent judicial review of other disputes over what should or should not be published. Already, much has been achieved. There is an overlapping series of professionally produced newspapers, national, regional and plant journals, the AS bulletin, tape cassettes, better coverage in the official media, formal access to television and radio, all of which ensures that the Polish workers now have their own source of information to rely on. This should not be got out of perspective. Most people anywhere in the world still only have time for a hasty glance at a newspaper and get most of their news from the television. Solidarity activists apart, Poles who rely on newspapers and television continue to get a partisan, incomplete account of what is happening in the political, economic and social fields of Polish society and are simply not informed about what the union is doing and saying. Despite the improvements since August 1980, the Polish mass media are no better than most Western media in reporting the activities of workers and their unions. As Solidarity continues to push and probe the limits of State control of information and the media, it is raising questions about the nature of public information, news reporting and publishing policy that have never been satisfactorily answered in the most progressive and liberal of the Western democracies, let alone in a self-proclaimed Socialist State. A movement towards a wider, more honest and accurate plurality of information is essential if Solidarity is to attempt to fulfil the hope placed in it. As Janusz Gorny, a young computer technician in Katowice told me: "We simply don't have enough data on which to make decisions. We know Poland is in an economic mess, but if we don't know how much is spent on the health service or how much is spent on internal security or even what the national income really is, how can we decide what our economic priorities should be?"

Chapter 11

Poland and the Workers of the World

The Trades Union Congress in Britain always holds its annual conference in the first week of September. When the thousand delegates assembled in Brighton for the 1980 TUC meeting they found the TUC's leadership in a thoroughly embarrassing position over Poland. The TUC's economic department had organised a trip to Poland to discuss the problem of cheap Polish imports with the official trade union body (CRZZ) in Warsaw. The delegation led by David Basnett, General Secretary of the powerful General and Municipal Workers' Union and a former TUC Chairman, was due to go to Poland in the week after the TUC conference. The arrangements had been made in April 1980, long before the revolt of the Gdansk workers. Now, delegates wanted to know if the delegation would still go ahead, if they would continue to meet the clearly irrelevant and discredited CRZZ official union, and why they would not instead travel to Gdansk to meet Lech Walesa. The tension over what the TUC would do was heightened by the speech at the beginning of the Congress by the fraternal delegate from the United States' AFL-CIO, America's equivalent of the TUC. Normally the AFL-CIO fraternal delegate's speech is an unremarkable, anodyne affair, but this time he included a passage in his speech which strongly praised the Polish workers' strike. "I think", he said, "that perhaps we are on the eve of a small miracle, namely, the right of workers to choose unions of their own, uninhibited by the interference of government or government-controlled trade unions." There was a burst of applause from delegates seated in different parts of the hall at this condemnation of the official trade unions in Poland, the official trade unions that the TUC delegation was due to meet in a few days' time.

In fact the TUC had not issued any statement of support for the Polish strikers and its public indifference to what had been happening in Gdansk since 14th August 1980 had been the object of considerable criticism in British trade union circles. The row over the Polish trip rumbled on during the week of the TUC conference, only finally ending when the CRZZ sent a message saying the trip would be turned into a one-day affair, with no opportunity to visit Gdansk or meet any of the leaders of the striking workers. Shortly afterwards, the Polish embassy cancelled the visit, and both

Basnett and the TUC Chairman, Tom Jackson, made strong statements of support for the Poles' right to form their own independent trade unions.

While the TUC was trying to sort out the problems caused by its lack of certainty on how to handle the workers' revolt in Poland, trade union bodies in other countries were firmly lining up behind the Polish strikers and their demands. In France, the socialist CFDT, sent a delegation to Gdansk and presented 15,000 French francs to Lech Walesa. The American AFL-CIO strongly supported the strike, while North American steelworkers and autoworkers organised plant collections for the strikers. Messages of support flowed into Gdansk from third world countries where unions saw many similarities between their own struggle and what was going on in Poland. The International Metalworkers' Federation, representing 14 million workers, sent a telegram to Walesa stating: "Workers in shipyards all over the world are anxiously watching developments in Poland in the hope that not only your fully just demands are met, but that your desire for independent trade union organisation, free of Party and State control, can be turned into reality. If there is any practical solidarity or financial help that we can provide, please let us know."

The differing responses from various trade union bodies in the West were no more than reflections of their previous attitudes to workers' struggles in Eastern Europe. Western unions that had tried to build relationships with official trade unions in Eastern Europe under the détente policies of the 1970's were confused as to how to make contact with the striking workers, and did not know whether the existence of Solidarity meant that all relations with the CRZZ unions in Poland should now be broken off. Unions that had supported Polish workers, KOR, and efforts by workers in Russia, Rumania and Czechoslovakia to build independent trade unions now felt that support to be fully justified. Other unions whose international policy was chiefly conditioned by a fanatical *anti*-communist, rather than a *pro*-workers position, hailed the Gdansk Agreement more as a blow against the Soviet Union than a victory for the Polish working class.

Well-intentioned pro-détente union leaders from Western Europe who had stayed in the plush Black Sea resorts provided for the favoured guests of East European trade unions, now had to ask themselves some awkward questions about the nature of official trade unionism in those countries, and how far their hosts were genuinely representative of the workers. Trade union officials who were members of, or close to, Communist Parties, kept their mouths shut at the sight of workers so decisively rejecting communist-run official trade unions. The few who criticised the

Polish workers looked extremely stupid. Meanwhile, other trade union leaders who had ruthlessly purged rank and file dissidents in their own unions and who had rarely, if ever, endorsed strikes by their own membership, let alone workplace occupations, were now singing the praises of the occupiers of the Lenin Shipyard and of Lech Walesa, by any standards an anti-bureaucracy dissident. Western trade unionists can find in Solidarity whatever best suits their ideological outlook. Right-wingers hail the threat to Soviet control of Eastern Europe now posed by Solidarity, while left-wingers welcome its ultra-democratic style.

At first sight the international trade union movement seems neatly divided into two giant trade union blocs reflecting the division between the communist and non-communist world. There is the International Confederation of Free Trade Unions (ICFTU) in Brussels, which has the major Western trade union organisations, like the British TUC, the West German DGB and the Swedish LO, in membership; and there is the World Federation of Trade Unions (WFTU) in Prague to which all the communist-controlled national trade union centres belong. But there are major differences of opinion between Western trade union national centres, and the biggest of them, the United States AFL-CIO, is not even a member of the ICFTU. (It is likely that the AFL-CIO will rejoin the ICFTU in late 1981). The AFL-CIO, in turn, has a sharply different international policy from the Canadian Labor Congress, even though there are many North American unions which belong to both national centres. The Western international trade union scene is further complicated by the existence of International Trade Union Secretariats, which group individual national trade unions on an industrial basis (so unions organising steelworkers, autoworkers, electrical industry workers and shipyard workers belong to the International Metalworkers' Federation, while miners' unions belong to the International Federation of Miners).

The International Trade Union Secretariats pursue policies that do not always coincide with those of the ICFTU or any single national trade union centre. On many issues such as South Africa, Latin America, North-South development, and energy, there are bitter political divisions between the various components of the non-communist international trade union movement and equally there have been varying responses to the creation and growth of Solidarity.

Solidarity and Western Trade Unions

It was to the complicated and confusing world of international trade unionism that Solidarity turned for support. As Mieczyslaw Gil, chairman of the 750,000-strong Cracow region of Solidarity told a Washington press conference when he led the first Solidarity delegation to visit the United States for the International Metalworkers' Federation 1981 World Congress: "We need the moral support of all trade unions outside of Poland." Although some Polish trade union activists had tried to make contact with Western trade unions prior to 1980, notably Kazimierz Switon in Silesia, the contact had been limited. Two journals, *Labour Focus on Eastern Europe,* published in London, and *L'Alternative,* published in Paris, provided detailed information on the activities of the opposition trade union movement and KOR, but neither journal had a very wide circulation amongst British or French trade unionists. The problems of language, contacts, getting visas and the general lack of information about Poland meant that few Western trade unionists felt moved to seek out direct contact with workers in Poland who were interested in creating a new kind of workers' movement. After August 1980 Solidarity did not have to reach out for contacts with Western trade unions; instead it was deluged with letters, invitations and visits from Western trade unions and international trade union federations. In a world in which workers were everywhere on the defensive and that had recently elected two extreme reactionaries as heads of government in Britain and the United States, the Polish workers' struggle caught the imagination of trade unions everywhere.

After August 1980 there was a stream of trade union visitors from outside Poland trying to find out what was happening and get more detailed information on Solidarity's organisation. Leaders of the Japanese Shoyo Federation came as early as September 1980, while in December 1980 Edmond Maire, General Secretary of the French CFDT, went to Warsaw and Gdansk and met Lech Walesa and other Solidarity leaders. Michael Mullen, General Secretary of the Irish Transport and General Workers' Union, led an official delegation to visit Solidarity in May 1981. On the other hand, in April 1981, Herman Rebhan, General Secretary of the International Metalworkers' Federation, was refused a visa by the Polish government, despite having a written invitation from Solidarity. The head of the International Department of the West German metalworkers' union, IG Metall, was abruptly ordered to leave Poland after he had spent a week visiting Solidarity offices. In the early days of the new union a delegation from the Institute for Workers' Control, including a British Labour MP, was refused entry visas to Poland. While the Polish government placed difficulties in the way of senior Western trade union representatives visiting Poland, it was possible for workers and trade union officials not holding senior positions to enter Poland on tourist visas. The relative freedom inside the country to move around and either stay in hotels or private homes, meant that contacts could be made at all levels with Solidarity without the Polish authorities taking too much interest.

Taking the Message Outside Poland

Slowly Solidarity responded to the invitations it received and started to send more delegations abroad. Walesa made a well publicised visit to Rome in January 1981 to see both the Pope and the Italian trade union confederations. Later on he visited Japan, and in March 1981 he had to cancel at the last minute a visit to France at the CFDT's invitation because of the crisis that broke out over the Bydgoszcz incident. Bogdan Lis, one of Solidarity's top leaders, paid an official visit to the TUC and British trade unions in March 1981. He met Len Murray and the TUC's International Committee; he visited the Executive Council of the Amalgamated Union of Engineering Workers and spoke to shop stewards at the General and Municipal Workers' Union's education college. He also met Transport and General Workers' Union as well as the Electrical and the Postal Workers' leaders. By now the TUC and most British unions had moved to a position of open support for Solidarity. Lis was impressed by the warmth of the welcome he received, and especially by the amount of time Len Murray spared for him. However, there is one point Solidarity leaders always find irritating when making contact with trade union leaders abroad, and that is the constant reference to possibilities of Soviet invasion and Poland's delicate geo-political situation. As Lis said when he returned to Gdansk: "When I saw Len Murray I wanted to talk about how one builds up trade unions; he kept on talking about the TUC's concern about the dangers to world peace if anything should go wrong in Poland".

Other delegations went to Sweden, France, Spain, Switzerland and Belgium in 1981. Solidarity representatives had become a familiar sight at the summer conferences of several British unions, including the GMWU and NALGO, the 700,000-strong local government officers' union. The Solidarity delegation attending the French CFDT Metalworkers' Congress at La Rochelle in February 1981 was enthusiastically welcomed by the singing of the *International* and the waving of clenched fists. The look of dismay on the Poles' faces at hearing what was to them the tune of the Russian national anthem and the symbol of communist one-party rule, was eloquent testimony to the cultural distance between Polish and French workers. Solidarity also looked beyond Europe. Andrzej Gwiazda, Walesa's deputy, took part in a ICFTU conference for Asian unions in New Delhi. Each of these visits helped to cement Solidarity's existence as part of the world trade union movement.

The strengthening of contacts with trade union movements in countries such as Britain and Sweden which had maintained close relationships with trade unions in other East European countries was useful, as both British and Scandinavian trade union leaders quietly passed messages to the WFTU headquarters in Prague that any threat to Solidarity's existence would completely jeopardise all future contact between Western trade unions and WFTU trade unions.

An important taboo was broken in May 1981, when the first Solidarity delegation to visit the United States landed in New York. They came as official observers at the 25th World Congress of the International Metalworkers' Federation. Their participation had been the subject of negotiations between Solidarity and the Polish government, with the latter strongly objecting to Solidarity going to the United States. Solidarity countered by saying that, as an independent union it would decide what visits to make and what to refuse. The government backed off and a four-person delegation took part in the IMF Congress. With trade unions from more than sixty countries taking part in the Congress, it was an excellent opportunity for the Solidarity delegation to exchange views with workers and trade union officials from countries in Africa, Asia and Latin America. The Solidarity delegation had a long meeting with black trade unionists from South Africa, and as the white Poles talked to the black South Africans about the pre-August 1980 problems in the building of effective independent trade unions, they found that they were describing many experiences common to workers in both countries. Following a visit to a Baltimore steel plant to talk to fellow steelworkers, the Poles met Doug Fraser, president of the American autoworkers' union, who invited Solidarity to send a delegation of workers from Polish tractor factories and auto plants to visit equivalent plants in the United States and Canada.

The integration of Solidarity as the internationally recognised labour organisation representing Polish workers was further underlined by Lech Walesa's participation as the official Polish workers' representative at the annual meeting of the International Labour Organisation held in Geneva in June 1981. The ILO brings together all the members of the United Nations, who have to send tri-partite delegations consisting of government, employer and worker representatives. In 1981, for the first time in more than thirty years at the ILO, the workers' representative from an East European State would be someone who had not been chosen by the Communist Party or the government. Solidarity also reckoned that the strict application of ILO conventions, especially those concerning the right to organise and strike, would be useful international benchmarks in safeguarding the gains made by Polish workers after August 1980.

Solidarity's statutes make clear that it has no formal foreign policy. It supports Poland's socialist system and the alliances — i.e. the Warsaw Pact — which Poland has with other countries. In addition, according to Professor Bronislaw Geremek, Solidarity's senior expert adviser on international policy, the union's "field of conflict is to do with internal problems. We don't want to transfer our conflict on to the international level. Solidarity should not try to form fixed international policy ideas too quickly. This is a delicate field where we have to advance step by step. We want bilateral relations with all the unions and confederations without having any special preference, save that we keep a warm spot in our hearts for those who sent us help during the Gdansk strikes and the early days of Solidarity. Obviously we feel happier with unions and confederations that support our ideas that unions should be independent and self-governing, but we are not making any political preferences." Solidarity representatives have tried to get in touch with WFTU headquarters in Prague, but have received no reply to their letters. The Soviet Union controls the WFTU decision-making process, and it will be interesting to see if there is any attempt by the WFTU to recreate relations with Polish workers in order to try and counter the deepening contacts Solidarity is making with trade unions in non-communist countries.

Practical Help From Outside Poland

In May 1981, I was standing in the grubby rooms that serve the Solidarity headquarters in Gdansk as a printing centre. Two tabletop offset duplicators were being worked at full speed, but one of the printers sadly pointed to a new duplicator that had been sent to Gdansk by a European trade union. "It's a very good machine, and one of our regional offices could certainly use it. But it only takes a certain kind of stencil and once they have run out, the machine will be useless," he said. A similar story can be told all over Poland of equipment being sent as gifts from Western trade unions and not being able to be used because of parts or ink running out, or lack of operator knowledge. Despite these problems, Solidarity has had a life-line to trade unions outside Poland which has provided the new union with essential printing equipment. Despite accusations in *Pravda* of Solidarity being financed by Western trade union money and the rather stupid statements by some Western trade union spokespersons in the early days of the Gdansk strike in which they talked loosely of sending money to the Poles, there has been no actual transfer of foreign currency into Poland for Solidarity's use. Firstly, Solidarity does not need the cash. Its membership dues provide it with a sufficient income inside Poland. The problem is that it cannot buy any of the printing equipment that it has always so badly needed, with its own income. All over Eastern Europe the sale of printing equipment — typewriters, duplicators, offset machines, photocopiers, electronic typesetting composers, plus paper, ink and printing chemicals — is extremely tightly controlled. You cannot go to a shop or a wholesaler, or even the manufacturer, and order and pay for such goods. So from the start Solidarity appealed to Western trade unions to send all kinds of printing equipment.

In September 1980 the AFL-CIO channelled $50,000 through Stockholm, where it was used to ship over some duplicators to Gdansk. The International Metalworkers' Federation and the Post and Telegraph Trade Union International (PTTI) bought a photocopier for the new union's headquarters in Gdansk. The French CFDT sent in two tons of paper and other office equipment. Visitors would arrive in Poland with cassette recorders or portable typewriters and leave them behind in Solidarity offices. The process was haphazard and unco-ordinated but, in a makeshift way, the various pieces of printing equipment sent in by Western trade unions found their way to different Solidarity offices and were put to good use. In January 1981 the ICFTU set up a co-ordinating office in Stockholm.

There was an unnecessary controversy over a Pole living in exile in Sweden who was appointed by the ICFTU as a liaison man with Solidarity, but whom the Swedish LO (the LO is Sweden's equivalent of the TUC) refused to work with, on the grounds of his links with KOR. Given the Swedish trade union movement's co-operation with political exiles from other countries, some people thought their action was a touch churlish. The Swedes brought over some Solidarity members to be trained in printing techniques and, by early Summer 1981, were shipping over to Poland enough equipment to set up a modest print shop. Both Solidarity and Western trade unions realised that it was necessary to keep open as many routes as possible into Poland for printing equipment. The IMF continued to send advanced electronic typewriters and composers directly into Poland, while French trade unions tried to send in lorry loads of material. The French metalworkers in the CFDT also gave two cars, donated by Peugeot and Renault workers to a visiting delegation of Solidarity members in February 1981.

It is difficult to put an accurate figure on the total value of the printing equipment sent into Poland by the trade union movement in other parts of the world. The TUC launched an appeal for a fund of £20,000 ($40,000), while the Swedish LO promised £60,000 ($120,000). The IMF has helped to organise the despatch of printing equipment bought with money collected by its affiliates (which include the world's more powerful and rich unions) to the value of about £50,000 ($100,000). In May 1981 the AFI-CIO *News* reported that American unions had raised $250,000 (£120,000). Many unions have sent smaller gifts or secondhand printing equipment. The total value of printing equipment actually sent to Poland, up to mid-1981, would be something over £200,000 ($400,000). It sounds a lot until you divide it into Solidarity's 8 – 10 million members, and if you consider that each year the TUC alone pays more than that in affiliation fees to the ICFTU. The flow of printing equipment and other goods demanded by Solidarity has been of great help to the Polish workers and has demonstrated in a practical way a form of international trade union solidarity. But the Western trade union movement has neither financed Solidarity nor have the goods sent into Poland provided more than 15 per cent of Solidarity's printing capacity. In one respect the Western trade unions have been relatively helpless to fulfil a demand made by Solidarity: that is for training courses for Solidarity organisers in areas such as collective bargaining, trade union organisation and workplace health and safety. Although there have been offers from Western unions to organise basic trade union training courses, either in Poland or in West European countries, the Polish government has discouraged all efforts by Polish trade unionists to involve trade unions outside Poland in training programmes.

At the Gdansk national headquarters there is a full time international department headed by Jacek Korczynski. The Solidarity national praesidium member responsible for international relations is Ryszard Kalinowski. The two of them made a long trip through France, Belgium and Italy in May 1981, trying to gain more information about what Western trade unions could do to help Solidarity. They found that Solidarity was being used in many of the fights between different trade union groupings in the non-communist world. A minor international trade union confederation called the World Confederation of Labour (WCL) whose members consist of the remnants of what had formerly been the confessional Christian unions, had as its General Secretary a Pole, Jan Kulakowski. Kulakowski was a close personal friend of Tadeusz Mazowiecki, an important Solidarity adviser. For a while it looked as if Kulakowski, who had few visa problems in entering Poland, was overly influencing Solidarity's international policy in favour of his own confederation, even though none of the really important unions in Western Europe and North America belonged to it. But the continuing flow of equipment and visits and, most importantly, the commitment by Western unions to provide help that Solidarity requested without any ideological strings attached helped to convince Solidarity of the need to maintain good relations with the groups that could best help the new union.

For any trade union organisation, developing a successful and honourable international policy is difficult. Solidarity has picked its way through the minefield of international trade union relationships without too many false steps. Polish workers have built personal links with trade unions and workers in other countries which have increased the interest and involvement of workers outside of Poland in the fate of Solidarity. At a time when many national trade union movements were preaching an isolationist economic policy, or were concentrating increasingly on defensive national solutions which ignored the needs or the plight of workers in other countries, the arrival of the new trade union of Polish workers who cried out for moral and practical support, was a timely reminder of the need and the usefulness of international workers' solidarity.

Chapter 12

The Workers and the Party

The Central Committee of the Polish United Workers' Party (Poland's Communist Party) that met in the second week of June 1981, was in an unenviable position. It had to digest the contents of a letter it had received from its sister Central Committee of the Communist Party of the Soviet Union, which explicitly criticised the failure of First Secretary Kania and Premier Jaruzelski to crack down on Solidarity and put an end to Poland's newly-found sense of freedom. The Soviet letter was couched in identical terms to the letter sent to the Communist Party leadership in Czechoslovakia a few days before the Soviet invasion in 1968. While much Western attention has focused on the possibility of a military intervention by the Soviet Union, it has sometimes been overlooked that the Kremlin has tremendous economic power over Poland and, by simply withdrawing or lessening the flow of credit, energy, raw materials, or by denying Poland markets, the Soviet leadership could quickly plunge Poland into a state of almost total economic and social chaos.

If the pressure from Moscow was almost unbearable for the Central Committee, then the pressure from the base of the Polish Party was equally difficult to cope with. Of the Polish Communist Party's 3.2 million members, it is reckoned that up to 1.5 million are members of Solidarity. During the 4-hour warning strike by all Solidarity members on 27th March 1981, the Party issued an instruction to all its members to stay at work. The instruction was completely ignored. A quarter of the Party's membership is in Poland's 168 largest factories — the factories where Solidarity has its strongest presence and organisation. During the Central Committee meeting an anti-Solidarity speaker complained that 30 per cent of the delegates elected for the extraordinary Party Congress, due to take place in 1981, were members of Solidarity, whereas only 22 per cent were workers. One of his colleagues said: "Perhaps they are the same people". He was probably right. As one Solidarity leader told me: "I don't think it has ever been a question of the Party infiltrating its people into Solidarity. Rather more a question of Solidarity members taking over the Party!"

The rank and file membership of the Party had been calling for some kind of reform ever since the creation of Solidarity. Just as the new union unleashed new forces which changed much of Poland's life well beyond the workplace, so too, it provoked immense changes inside the Party itself. There were calls for democratic and secret elections to be held at the base which, in many cases, produced new delegates to different Party bodies. The central nature of all Soviet-inspired Communist Parties is democratic centralism which, very roughly, means that Party posts are filled from the top down and policy decisions, once made, have to be unquestionably carried out. This vertical structure was challenged by increasing horizontal contacts between Party members at the same level, but living in different parts of Poland. The exact extent and influence of this horizontal movement is difficult to make out. Too many conclusions have been drawn from only one or two meetings in cities such as Torun, or the over-excited interviews given by some Party members advocating horizontalism. Party members may well elect new people in order to remove those who have been in charge in the disastrous 1970's, but it is in the nature of most political processes to choose a cautious centrist in whom trust can be placed, in preference to a radical demagogue. As the Solidarity elections held in the Summer of 1981 suggest, the more outspoken of the 1980 strike leaders were being replaced by more moderate candidates. If this was true for Solidarity, then it was even more true for the Polish Communist Party, which wanted change, but not at a price that brought outside intervention or a lessening of its own power in Polish society. (At times it is almost possible to feel sorry for the Polish Communist Party. It is attacked by Solidarity for not being liberal enough, and savaged by the Kremlin for conceding far too much. It is reviled by other East European leaders and scorned in the West for its economic and political incompetence. Meanwhile, it is the only Communist — and ruling — Party that Poland has, and both Party and the people have somehow to learn to live with each other).

The Central Committee meeting in June saw a hard-fought battle between those who wanted to ditch Kania and Jaruzelski and return to a Poland where workers knew their place and were kept in it, and those who had opted for a process of renewal. In the words of Mieczyslaw Rakowski, the Vice-Premier in charge of negotiations with Solidarity: "We must not forget that the Polish Communist Party answers to history for the bloodshed in Poznan and the Baltic Coast. We cannot have that happen again and our Party would not survive if it did. The Soviet comrades", Rakowski continued, "have the right to present their criticisms, and our internationalist obligation is to study them carefully and to draw conclusions, but doing so while taking into account our national specificity and the concrete political situation we face". By dint of some skilful procedural manoeuvring that would do credit to a sophisticated Western political operator, Kania outflanked his opponents and survived to another day. But he was still faced with trying to square the circle of Moscow pressure, the existence of Solidarity and the deep divisions within the Party itself.

Solidarity and Politics

Solidarity itself claims no political ambitions. Again and again, Lech Walesa and other Solidarity leaders have proclaimed that Solidarity is a trade union not a political movement. National Co-ordinating Commission member Mieczyslaw Gil put it this way: "Our union has almost ten million members and, together with their families, this constitutes more than half of Poland's population of 36 million. This means that our actions have a tremendous impact on the economic and social life of our country. Our union, which out of necessity, has the features of a mass social movement, has to take care of the whole nation's interests. We have to defend and promote the human rights, the citizens' rights and the workers' rights of all our members. But let me stress: we have no political ambitions."

Gil is perfectly correct. Solidarity has no political programme. It does not seek to organise a Party in the way, for example, that the British trade union movement set up the Labour Party at the beginning of this century. It does not sponsor candidates for any elections. Its own propaganda acknowledges the leading role of the Communist Party. Although critical of the economic organisation of the country, no-one in the union has called for the dismantling of the State ownership of the means of production. In talks with workers in several different factories I never met one who thought that returning to private ownership would solve any problems. A headline in the Szczecin Solidarity newspaper *Jednosc* summed up the political feeling inside Solidarity: "Progressive Socialism — Yes. Distortions — No!" Although Solidarity permits Communist Party members to take leading roles in the union, and some like Bogdan Lis in Gdansk and Marian Jurczyk in Szczecin, hold very senior positions in the national leadership, it has a rule in its statutes which expressly forbids anyone who holds an elected Solidarity post from being an office holder in either the Party or local administration. This may seem strange in comparison with trade unions outside Poland where officials are often councillors or local magistrates, but in Solidarity the need to separate clearly trade union office from the political, State and judicial apparatus is seen to be essential.

It is precisely this point that most unsettles the Communist Party in Poland, and especially in the Soviet Union. In declaring itself to be, and ensuring through its statutes that it is, a trade union completely apart from the power structure that existed in Poland up to August 1980, Solidarity made a profoundly important political point. It is nothing short of seeking a separation of powers in a State where only one source of power is permitted to exist. In part, this reflected a dislike, many Poles would say hatred, for the Polish Communist Party. Too many of its leading office holders, in too many regions of Poland, were associated with corruption or with arbitrary and malicious acts and decisions. The corruption was very real. Concrete, wood and steel would be diverted from industrial projects to build dachas for leading Party functionaries. While Poland desperately needed hospitals and kindergartens, money was easily found to build new Party offices in many regions.* A chance evening visit to any of the big Orbis hotels in Poland's major cities would usually reveal expensive receptions attended by Party functionaries, where the food and drink available existed only in the dreams of the average Pole. Party members secured many advantages in the workplace and community — quicker access to car purchase, better education for their children, bigger apartments.

The Nomenklatura

Then there was, and still is, the *nomenklatura*. *Nomenklatura* is a Russian word meaning those people who are named to their post. It is the system of *nomenklatura* that permits a single Party to exercise control over so much of political, social, economic, educational and cultural organisation in the East European States. Any position of power or authority in Poland will be filled by someone named to it by the Party, i.e. a member of the *nomenklatura*. It is not a haphazard process. In 1972 the Central Committee of the Polish Communist Party issued directives which listed the important *nomenklatura* positions at national, regional and district level. (See Appendix for full list). Ministers, top civil servants, diplomats, editors of newspapers, heads of scientific research institutes, chairmen of regional or district councils, all senior posts in the army and police, bank managers, hospital directors, presidents of the official trade unions, regional chairpersons of youth and veteran organisations, museum directors, university rectors, judges, director-generals of television and radio, fire brigade chiefs — all these public posts are part of the *nomenklatura*. Appointments, promotions and dismissals will be decided upon by the Party. It is therefore to the Party that the 100,000 members of the *nomenklatura* (100,000 is the figure officially cited in Poland, but

---

*Solidarity has forced regional and Party administrators to disgorge 118 buildings, which are now used as kindergartens or community centres.

Party influence over appointments can extend right down to junior managerial positions) look, for their place in the sun. *Nomenklatura* members, in addition to having good jobs, get other privileges such as foreign travel, or the opportunity for further training.

Like the adminstrative grade of the British Civil Service, members of the *nomenklatura* are considered to be general administrators, able to fill any post and easily switching from, say, supervising a foreign trade department, to overseeing the Polish television system. Their ideological outlook and loyalty to the establishment is more important than technical or managerial ability. Since August 1980 the Polish *nomenklatura* has been living very uneasily. In its top echelons there have been several reshuffles, but the bulk of the *nomenklatura* remains in place. The whole question of the *nomenklatura* was very gingerly handled during the negotiations leading up to the Gdansk Agreement. Point No. 13 of the Agreement claimed the following: "To introduce the principle of cadre selection on the basis of qualifications, not on the basis of membership of the Party". The government responded: "The demand for cadres to be selected on the basis of qualifications and ability has been accepted". And there the matter rested. In fact, the *nomenklatura* has been left relatively untouched. Appointments are still made by and through the Party. The *nomenklatura* is the web that holds together the Soviet-style communist organisation of society. Its dismantling or, at least, its orientation towards socially valid goals is one of the biggest problems in a reconstruction of Poland, or, indeed, any East European State.

Towards Political Reform

Previous reform movements that emerged from workers' revolts in Poland lost their impetus as workers' representatives became absorbed into the Party-State apparatus, and then were discarded once the push for reform died away. Solidarity seeks to guard itself against this possibility, by separating itself from all formal influence by the Party. As in the discussion over workers' self-management, this has sometimes led to a confusion over the extent to which the union can participate with the government in resolving political and economic problems. Should union experts, for example, sit on joint commissions, or should the government present proposals to which the union reacts? At what stage does discussing issues in a Warsaw ministry in a bid to reach consensus, become a process of incorporation?

According to Jacek Kuron, the Polish Communist Party and government need to withdraw from certain areas of social control, while retaining power over the army, police and central administration. It would not be a question of Solidarity filling all of the vacuum thus left, but rather a question of other groups in Polish society — the liberal professions, the academic world, the media, cultural institutions — gaining autonomy and operating within limitations laid down by the State, but free of the direct control exercised until now through Party domination of the *nomenklatura*. There seems general agreement that Poland's foreign policy and internal alliances would be removed from the political debating arena. This latter point is more easily wished for than achieved. The euphemism about not questioning "Poland's foreign policy and international alliances" actually means "we dare not say anything nasty about the Soviet Union". It is a difficult point to swallow for a country whose national cultural consciousness is deeply anti-Russian, and was anti-Russian long before it became anti-Soviet. The majority of Solidarity members have grandparents who lived in Poland under Tsarist rule. Many of Poland's plays, poems and other literature recount revolts against Russian rule. The Nazi-Soviet non-aggression pact of 1939, following which Hitler and Stalin carved up Poland between themselves, is not so far back in history that it can be easily forgotten. The undoubted suffering and heroism of the Russian people and the Red Army in making the major contribution to the defeat of Nazism is overshadowed by Polish resentment at the dominant role played by the Soviet Union in Poland since 1945. In addition to the obligatory transfer of Soviet political and economic models, there were crude and offensive interferences in Polish political life, such as the installing of the Russian Marshal Rokossovski as head of the Polish Army during the 1950's.

In Katowice the wall of a large building at the end of one of the main shopping streets is completely covered by a painting of a Polish flag and a Russian flag, side by side. Superimposed on the flags are two hands clasped in a handshake, and beside this image is the slogan: "Eternal alliance, brotherly friendship, comprehensive co-operation". These clumsy propaganda efforts to sell the Soviet Union to the Poles do not have any real impact. Still remembered is the death of 15,000 Polish officers which, following the discovery of mass graves at Katyn, most Poles blame on the Russians. Many Solidarity members in the Summer of 1981 were sporting badges with a cross and the word 'Katyn' on them and the Young Poland Movement were distributing posters and leaflets calling for a settling of accounts over Katyn. In June 1981 there was a spate of incidents in which memorials to the Soviet troops were defaced. The authorities blamed hot-headed youngsters, but some Solidarity members thought it could be a deliberate provocation organised by the Party in order to depict Poland sliding into open anti-

Sovietism. Lech Walesa, sensing the danger caused by these incidents, offered to go himself and clean up one such defaced memorial in Lublin, and regional Solidarity headquarters immediately sent out teams to scrub anti-Soviet slogans off the war memorials.

The union was thus caught in a dilemma. Having claimed a general liberalisation of Polish political life, it had no clear idea how far, or where exactly, it wanted to go. One example was the long campaign to secure the release of right-wing political prisoners belonging to the Confederation of Independent Poland. Headed by former journalist, Leszek Moczulski, whose book "Revolution Without a Revolution" argued for a removal of Poland from the Soviet sphere of influence and the introduction of political plurality, the Confederation had, prior to August 1980, organised demonstrations, attracting a few thousand people. Moczulski and four other leaders were arrested in August 1980, at the same time as KOR leaders. While the KOR people were released as part of the Gdansk settlement, Moczulski was left in prison. Solidarity took up a clear position. The union opposed what the Confederation stood for, but would fight against people being imprisoned for expressing their opinion. In December 1980 there was set up a Committee for the Defence of Prisoners of Conscience, having as members personalities in Polish life, as well as Solidarity leaders. It was an attempt by the union to create a campaigning body that would be clearly marked off and separate from Solidarity.

Faced with all its other problems in the Autumn and Winter of 1980 – 81, Solidarity took little action over the demand for the political prisoners' release. But, after the Bydgoszcz incident, pressure from the base mounted. Posters appeared demanding their release. Moczulski's wife and five workers in Sosnowiec started a hunger strike in protest at their continued detention. Again, the point of reference was the Gdansk Agreement. Point 4 claimed the release of all political prisoners and a halt to "repression against people for their opinions", to which the government agreed "to institute full liberty of expression in public and professional life". As in so many other areas the Gdansk Agreement haunted the government authorities as they continued to keep Moczulski and the other political prisoners in gaol. A meeting between Solidarity and the government on 27th April 1981 produced no result. The government side said that, if released, Moczulski would become dangerous. Zbigniew Przydzial, a Wroclaw member of Solidarity's National Co-ordinating Commission retorted that if Moczulski was dangerous now, why had he not been arrested before August 1980. Another Solidarity representative asked why the law was not being invoked against those who were shooting workers in 1970 and 1976.

Faced with this impasse, students at Warsaw University took matters into their own hands and organised a demonstration on 25th May through the centre of Warsaw. Other student marches were planned for Gdansk, Kielce and Katowice, but in response to requests from both Solidarity and the University authorities, were called off. Solidarity leaders disapproved of street demonstrations, but were ignored by the students. A procession, with Polish flags and banners, marched peacefully through Warsaw. The demonstration passed off without incident, but it showed that Solidarity could not, through the fiat of its leaders, control all the forces urging political change in Poland.

In fact the Polish authorities' handling of the Moczulski affair was disastrous. By first imprisoning him, and then refusing to release him, they turned a minor right-wing political figure into a semi-martyr. Amid considerable international publicity, he and his colleagues were released early in June 1981 to await their trial. To the Soviet Union it must have been almost inconceivable that the Polish government would thus give way. To Solidarity it seemed once again, that talking politely to the authorities did not achieve nearly as much as hunger strikes or street demonstrations. Students and the Young Poland Movement, both outside Solidarity's control, felt that they could widen the margin of political freedom by using methods that would never be tolerated in any other East European State.

The Moczulski affair symbolises the difficulties Solidarity finds itself in when considering what its political role should be. It is all very well to say that the union has no political ambitions, does not want to become a political party or replace the government. But how can the union, for example, demand freedom of expression, but deny that freedom to those of its members who want to talk about Katyn, or express less than brotherly love for the Soviet Union? It can ask its members to avoid discussion about the role of the Soviet Union, but it cannot compel them to stop treating this delicate subject. Solidarity often says that it wants to see the rule of law upheld, and in its protests over beatings-up or its demands for the bringing to justice those responsible for repression in 1970 and 1976, it often talks about the need for the law to be applicable to the authorities. Again, this is a fine liberal demand, but an effective and independent legal-judicial system that can guarantee individual rights presupposes a reduction of the power of the Communist Party that is scarcely compatible with existing concepts of democratic centralism. After August 1980, the Polish people had an alternative conduit for their political demands in the shape of Solidarity. There was plenty of loose talk about making Poland more democratic and more free, but little hardheaded analysis of what kind or what extent of democracy or freedom was desirable or attainable. Poland's working class had made both a political and an economic breakthrough in securing an independent trade union, but the existence of Solidarity raised political questions that at times seemed almost better left unanswered.

Chapter 13

The Future?

Peering through the crystal ball at Poland's future offers at best only a cloudy, unclear vision, with a continuing sense that a fit of old men's bad temper in the Kremlin could, anyway, smash it to pieces. The creation of an authentic, independent, democratically accountable and democratically controllable trade union, Solidarity, has changed nearly all the relationships — economic, social, political — that existed prior to August 1980. That process of change has not finished yet, and it is unlikely to terminate of its own accord for some time to come. Solidarity is the first mass workers' movement to develop without a theoretical base. The action came first and the theory has been developed afterwards. Some might say that this is the union's greatest strength — it has not had to carry loads of ideological luggage or twist its decisions to fit a given political theory.

The construction of a trade union model cannot be done at a desk, it can only be working out in practice. That working-out is continuing. In the Summer 1981 elections in some Solidarity regions, notably its biggest region around Warsaw, industrial workers were not being elected to regional committees. Instead, white collar workers and intellectuals were being chosen. Even in the Ursus tractor factory, stronghold of the industrial blue-collar membership of Solidarity in Warsaw, there was a majority of white-collar workers elected on to the plant praesidium. The link-up between intellectuals (in the broad Polish sense of the word) and workers was one of the most positive aspects of Solidarity's birth. According to Warsaw University sociologist, Jacek Kurczewski, who is one of the group of twenty-five national advisers to Solidarity, a "new middle class" has arisen in Poland "composed of skilled workers, relatively well-paid and educated, and the skilled 'white collars' or intellectuals and specialists that had not been given an adequate role in the decision-making process".

Discussing the role of intellectuals and white-collar workers, and their popularity as candidates in Solidarity elections, an Ursus worker responded: "We chose the best people. We don't worry if they are manual workers or if they have university degrees. It's what they say and stand for that counts, and whether we can trust them". This sounds very fine, but it is not impossible to see a situation developing where the effective Solidarity leadership no longer comes from the industrial working class, but rather consists of intellectuals and activists who, no matter their personal popularity, do not have the same outlook or sense of confidence based on an understanding of their own strength that industrial workers have. In the words of Irena Lewandowska, one of the team producing Warsaw Solidarity's daily bulletin *Niezaleznosc* (Independence): "workers often have more imagination than intellectuals". The case usually cited is the Gdansk negotiations where none of the experts who arrived in Gdansk to help the strikers, believed that the government could accept the creation of an independent trade union. Even Jacek Kuron says that it was perhaps a good thing that he was in prison during the Gdansk discussions. "If I had gone there I would have told them expecting to get independent trade unions was too much. I really believed it was impossible. In fact, I knew it was impossible". Yet the impossible happened, because the workers insisted on it.

Workers and Intellectuals

At the same time one must guard against romanticising each desire and act of the Polish workers. The link-up with intellectuals after 1976 was the key that unlocked the frustration of the Polish working class. The help of intellectuals since August 1980 has contributed immeasurably to the success of Solidarity. All the major Solidarity regions have Centres for Social Research attached to them, which group experts from local universities and the technical colleges. But the intellectuals must avoid the trap of substituting themselves for working-class leaders. This is undoubtedly what both the hardliners and the reformers in the Communist Party are hoping for. To see a growing gulf between the industrial base of Solidarity and the leadership over-dominated by intellectuals is the dream of Kania and Olszowski. One British journalist, writing in June 1981, described Solidarity as being increasingly in the hands of "jobless activists working as full-time union organisers", (how one can have full-time work and be jobless at the same time is a matter of debate for the journalist and his sub-editor), with the implication that this was an unhealthy development. On the contrary, the involvement of activists in Solidarity is in the best traditions of the creation of trade unions. If one looks at the history of the first years of trade unions in Britain, the United States, or the rebirth of trade unions in West Germany after the war, it was thanks to the energy of activists who offered their services to the emerging unions that they were able to develop successfully. Even now, the best of the authentic, democratic unions organising strikes and working-class resistance in South Africa or in Latin America are led by a mixture of young workers and activists. Finding the correct blend of leadership that most accurately reflects the industrial base of Solidarity while using to maximum effectiveness the knowledge and ability of intellectuals and activists is a continuing task for the union.

It remains a continuing task because the union is in a state of flux. The final structure is far from settled. There was talk in mid-Summer 1981 of reorganising the regional Solidarity structure into 26 basic units. Partly this was to concentrate sufficient logistical backup and expert advice for each regional centre, partly it was to exercise firmer control over the bushfire disputes and protests that were happening in smaller towns over which Solidarity as a whole had no control. The debate about a regional versus an industrial structure will continue to take place. In Western countries it has usually been industrial unions — the miners, the railwaymen, the steelworkers, the carworkers — that have been the strongest and best developed, and often politically the most progressive unions. Yet industrial unionism has weaknesses. It leaves weaker groups of workers without protection and increasingly as economies have developed their service and public sector industries it has become more difficult to unionise such workers. The growing work and influence of TUC regional councils in Britain suggests that finding common links between trade unionists on a geographical basis is seen as an important part of future trade union structural organisation in the country with the oldest and most traditional trade union movement in the world.

To some extent, workers in the major industries have taken matters into their own hands by starting an intense debate about self-management. Seminars, with representatives from the seventeen biggest enterprises — some of the biggest Polish steel works or ship yards, employing up to 50,000 workers — have been organised to discuss forms of self-management. Rather than wait for an economic reform package, workers are going ahead and drawing up their own plans for running plants. They are conscious of the mistakes of the workers' councils, set up after the Polish 'October' of 1956, and of the need to avoid incorporation. The key power being discussed is that of nominating and dismissing enterprise management. This removes some of the power the Party has to direct Poland's economy, and returns that power to the workers. A group of intellectuals in Szczecin produced this summary of the difference between State ownership and social ownership of the means of production: "The right to private property in the means of production was abolished in our country when production was put under State control. These facts are commonly accepted in Poland. The argument begins when official propaganda tells the entire na-

tion that in Poland the means of production are socially owned.
Theoretically, under socialism the means of production should be
held in common ownership by those who actually use them, that is,
the working class. But if the social ownership of the means of production is to be a true fact and not simply a propaganda statement,
then it involves control over one's own labour power, control and
the full right to decide on the social subject of that labour; it means
a structure of political and legal norms in harmony with the needs
of the world of labour. State ownership and social ownership of the
means of production are two completely different concepts which
should never be confused. The means of production may be owned
by the State, but this does not mean they are thereby the social property of the working class.''

A key clause in that statement refers to the need for ''a structure
of political and legal norms in harmony with the needs of the world
of labour''. Despite all the talks between Solidarity leaders and
government ministers, the draft bills, the special commissions, it is
difficult to say that the Polish government, and behind it, the
Polish United Workers' Party, has been ready to concede power in
the political and judicial field that would approach the kind of
political settlement wanted by Solidarity. The debate and struggle
within the Party, which was not even properly settled by the outcome of the extraordinary Party Congress in July 1981, will continue. Solidarity may be a trade union, but a union with nearly ten
million members is also a mass movement whose extremely wide
base is constantly pushing forward with new political demands. Ar-
ticulating these demands is difficult where an accurate and truthful
political language is simply not available. In a brilliant essay,
published in the *London Review of Books,* Michael Szkolny noted:
''The Polish words for 'socialism', 'socialisation' and 'internationalism' today designate respectively the existing social order,
State ownership and subordination to the interests of the Soviet
Union. The term 'anti-socialist force' is used to denote any form of
political opposition, while the word 'anarchist' is today reserved
for those oppositionists who belong to some current of the European socialist tradition. These examples form part of a general
phenomenon of conceptual embezzlement which reaches deep into
the vernacular. It is an Orwellian process, which fundamentally
limits people's conceptual framework. In consequence, these ideas
vanish deep into the collective subconscious, from which they
struggle to appear in periods of social crisis, often in the strangest
of new clothes.'' Solidarity's leaders, educated as they were under
post-1945 dispensation, have had difficulties in expressing exactly
what they want in language that was completely unambiguous.
Self-censorship is unavoidable. Certain subjects are taboo — the

leading role of the Party, the Soviet Union, the spread of independent trade unionism to other East European countries, but while such self-censorship, politically understandable and necessary as it may be, persists, then Solidarity's conceptual framework will remain limited.

The very existence of Solidarity and the blossoming of contacts with the West has been something of an object of wonder for trade unionists outside Poland. The fact that Walesa has been endlessly on our television screens, much like a Western trade union or political superstar has meant that the continuing insecurity of many Solidarity representatives has been not reported, or mentally shunted away as irrelevant, when mentioned in passing in newspaper reports. It is important to stress the problems of physical insecurity that besets many regions where Solidarity is not so strongly implanted, and where the party and militia never suffered that kind of humiliation experienced by the authorities in the regions where the victorious strikes of August and September 1980 took place. All during the Winter of 1981 there were too many attacks, beatings up, ransacking of offices, distribution of smear leaflets, arbitrary searches, for it to be put down to over-zealous local attempts to pressurise Solidarity. The attempts to arrest KOR leader Adam Michnik — he had to get a workers' guard for a period — meant that the authorities had not fully adjusted to Solidarity's existence. It is difficult to point to anything given freely by the authorities. Such freedoms that Solidarity has won since August 1980 it has had to take, often by pointing the pistol of a local, or even a national, strike, at the government's or Party's head. At the same time the authorities have tried to claw back what was negotiated away in Gdansk and it has needed industrial action or the effective threat of it to make them stay their hand.

A Quest for Stability

A constant plea by Polish workers is for some stability, a bit of peace and quiet, a few months without a major or even a minor crisis. It is difficult to see how they will arrive at this happy tranquility, given the present allocation of power in Poland. There is no steady state, no perfect equilibrium in which workers, unions, managements, political parties, governments, bureaucrats at all levels, each have a satisfactory sense of their own power. There is an unending struggle between labour and those who own the means of production, whether privately or by the State, and Solidarity cannot opt out of that struggle. What Lech Walesa, his chief advisers and the Church hope to do is make the struggle gradual, make it a process of debate and compromise and external arbitration rather than industrial attrition. Doubtless, there are many in

the leadership of the Party — sincere Polish patriots — who wish to
see a softening of the fight between Solidarity and the authorities.
But there is no evidence that the most liberal or reformist of the
Party leadership is willing to surrender voluntarily any effective
power. Radio Warsaw announced in May 1981 that since 1st
September 1980, 13 ministers, 40 deputy ministers, 18 provincial
governors, 26 deputy governors, 26 provincial Party first
secretaries, 72 provincial Party secretaries, 7 heads of central
departments and 14 directors of industrial groups had been "recalled from top posts". In addition, 8 members of the Sejm (Poland's
parliament) had been deprived of their mandate. In any other country, such an upheaval would be called a political revolution. In
Poland, cynics in Solidarity saw it as musical chairs. Without a fundamental reinstitutionalisation of Poland which would have to include a full acceptance of Solidarity, an independent judicial
system, greater media freedom, and some separation of political
and economic decision making, the country and its people would
still lurch unsatisfactorily along until either the great hopes of
August 1980 evaporated, or there was a cataclysmic showdown that
could end in disaster.

Solidarity, of course, wants to avoid either outcome. How it does
this is unclear. There is no blueprint for definitive change in
Poland. The workers' upheaval of 1980 is making new history. The
search for socialism and democracy in Poland is a difficult task. It
is difficult frankly, to see how it can be finally accomplished
without the involvement of workers in the Soviet Union and the
other East European states. The ruthless smashing of burgeoning
independent workers' movements in the Soviet Union and
Romania and the crackdown on left-wing intellectual critics of the
Czechoslovak and East German regines show how scared the rulers
of those countries are, of the kind of workers'-intellectuals' movement that gave birth to Solidarity. The slump in production in the
Soviet Union has meant that in recent years that country's rulers
can no longer deliver to its working class an increasing standard of
living and social protection. The Stalinist model of heavy and rapid
industrialisation which transformed Russia is no longer applicable
in the 1980's, and there is nothing to put in its place. On the black
market in West Russia, Solidarity badges and journals exchange
hands at high prices. A Polish train was refused admission to East
Germany because it was covered with Solidarity stickers. On the
Czechoslovakian border tourists from Poland are made to remove
their Solidarity badges. The fear of workers' freedom spreading
beyond Poland terrifies the Kremlin. So it should. Providing we
can prevent the White House and the Kremlin from taking their
arms race to its final conclusion it is a fairly safe bet that the only

hope for changing the Soviet Union for the better is for its industrial workers to being a process of repossessing power similar to that which has begun in Poland. How that will happen no-one knows. But then, even Jacek Kuron reckoned that the creation of an independent trade union in Poland was an impossibility.

Solidarity has to keep on working, keep on representing its members in the workplace, and outside it, keep on publishing its journals, bulletins and pamphlets, and keep on defending itself against attacks on what was conceded in the Gdansk Agreement. If it does this it will provide a basic trade union service which Polish workers have never had in their history. The continuing existence of Solidarity is itself an important part of the necessary changes in Poland. Lech Walesa correctly assesses the need to rap over the knuckles those of his members who demand specific, immediate changes and want the entire weight of the union placed behind those demands. The creation of socialist democracy involves choosing priorities and this Solidarity does in a more democratic way than most workers' organisations elsewhere in the world. In Daniel Singer's formulation the union has to prop up the outward shape of the Party because inside, its innards are being eaten away. Having begun a revolution in 1956, seen it repressed in 1970 and 1976, the Polish workers took the process a decisive stage further in 1980. And precisely because they have been so successful this stage is still difficult and dangerous, but full of hope — hope, not just for Polish workers, but for those trying to form effective, strong trade unions everywhere in the world. Solidarity knows that as it continues its work it will need all the help and advice that it can get from trade unions and workers outside Poland. Solidarity leaders understand very well that the union has plenty of what David Basnett called "false friends" in the West. The mendacity of Western Conservatives who share with Mr Brezhnev a common conception of trade unions — i.e. that they can be listed in the telephone book but are completely ineffective industrially — is fully appreciated in Poland. One should never confuse the warm welcome given by Solidarity representatives to Western visitors with a belief that they are swallowing all the rubbish that sometimes they politely sit through and hear.

Western trade unionists should be visiting Poland, arranging exchange visits, building direct workplace-to-workplace links, and building political and financial support for Solidarity in their own unions. In fact we have much to learn from Solidarity itself. Its openness, its democratic forms, its willingness to support issues beyond the workplace are all areas in which, perhaps, it has much more to teach the Western trade union movement than it has to learn from us. Polish workers believe in international solidarity because, as they put it, it is the best insurance "for your future, and for ours".

Appendices

APPENDIX I

The Charter of Workers' Rights — September 1979

Whereas:
— citizens are being deprived of the right to take part in decision making on matters that concern them;
— restrictions are being imposed on the fundamental rights of the employee, such as the right to safe and pensionable work, to a just wage, and to rest;
— social inequalities and injustices are becoming more profound;
— there exist no institutions to protect the employee — the official Polish Trade unions are not institutions of this kind;
— workers are denied their fundamental right of defence, which is the right to strike;
— society has to shoulder the cost of every mistake of the authorities, including the cost of the current crisis;

we have entered upon a course of action whose long-term aim is the creation of a self-defence system for employees, first and foremost, independent Trade Unions.

We wish to begin with the problems which seem to us to be capable of solution, at least in part, at the present time.

1. WAGES
— pay should rise at least in step with the cost of living; a cost of living supplement is essential;
— everyone should be ensured a minimum living wage; teams of specialists should work out this minimum and amend it in proportion to rising prices; families living below this line should be paid appropriate supplements;
— efforts must be made to eliminate glaring and unfounded differences in pay;
— stoppages of work, changes of quota, etc., must not be allowed to entail a drop in wages;
— workers doing the same job under the same conditions should receive remuneration in accordance with standardised scales of rates which are independent of the branch in which the said workers are employed.

2. WORKING HOURS
— it is inadmissible that overtime, additional and community work, should be compulsory; miners must have Sundays and holidays free;
— the **free Saturdays** of the current system must be legally guaranteed to everyone;
— efforts must be made to implement a **40-hour working week without reduction of wages.**

3. OCCUPATIONAL SAFETY
— safety standards and regulations must be observed **without exception;** there should be special commissions to monitor this, having wide powers, including the right to shut down a plant; commissions monitoring occupational health and safety, accident commissions and also factory doctors must be institutionally independent of the factory management;
— no-one who suffers loss of health due to harmful working conditions can be left without pay or income to which he is entitled;
— it is essential to update the current list of industrial diseases;
— **night work for women** must be eliminated; it should not be allowed that women do heavy physical work.

4. GRANTING OF PRIVILEGES
— the remuneration of an employee and his promotion should not depend on his Party allegiance, political opinions nor outlook;
— benefits such as bonus payments, housing or vacations must be allotted in an open manner; the means of allotting these goods and the names of the beneficiaries must be openly announced;
— there must be an end to the granting of privileges to groups connected with the government (police, Party functionaries): special allowances of goods greatly in demand, such as housing, plots of land, building materials, cars, special medical care, luxury holiday homes, special pension rights, etc.

5. COMPULSION TO ACT AGAINST ONE'S CONSCIENCE
— no-one should be forced to immoral acts, to inform for the Party or the security service, to take part in attacks on undesirable persons;
— people should not be compelled to produce shoddy goods, to carry out work which threatens their safety and that of others, to hush up accidents, make false reports, etc.

LABOUR CODE
The Labour Code in force since 1975 must be radically changed. It established regulations which are disadvantageous to the workers. Its articles are equivocal, and hence in any given situation can be and frequently are interpreted to the benefit of the management. In particular:
— Article 52 must be changed. It is used as an anti-strike law (the numerous sackings after June 1976 were based on it); the right to strike must be **guaranteed by law;**
— if someone is dismissed, the management must explain in writing the

reason for the dismissal; the worker should continue in his job so long as his case is going through the successive legal instances; throughout the whole process he should have the right to the assistance of a lawyer;
— union officials elected by the work force must be legally protected against dismissal for a certain time after laying down office also.

We consider that the realisation of these postulates depends on our own stance. Evidence that workers can force the authorities and management to make concessions is provided by the great showdowns of 1956, 1970 and 1976, and by individual strikes.

For several months now we have felt the effects of the crisis on our own skin. Deliveries and transport get worse and worse, wages are going down, prices are going up, in big plants the working hours are getting longer and are taking up the 'free Saturdays', there are more and more stoppages. If we ourselves do not now make a start at defending our own interests, our situation will go from bad to worse.

However, in order to win, we must rid ourselves of any feeling of impotence, stop passively putting up with restrictions on our rights and the deterioration of the conditions of life, and must look for the most effective form of action. There exist a great number of possibilities.

A. Undoubtedly the most effective form of action is to strike, even if the strikes are not on a large scale. Generally however, it is only effective in the short run. In order not to waste the achievements of a strike, the participants must elect representatives to monitor the realisation of their demands. If the workers know how to act in solidarity and are not afraid, they can force management to concessions by the very threat of a strike, by presenting petitions, or sending delegations.

B. A very great deal can be achieved simply by the dissemination of information. It is necessary to speak up loudly and to protest when someone is wronged, when we see injustice; it is necessary to publicise the actions of cliques and the granting of privileges, shortcomings and wastage, breaches of the regulations on occupational health and safety, and the hushing-up of accidents. It is necessary to speak about this to colleagues and at meetings. To demand that the authorities take a stand on this. To tell the independent social institutions and the independent press.

C. There are many problems in labour relations which can be solved by using the official trade unions. It would certainly be better for us if these were not dead as, in fact, they are at present. We must demand that the factory councils defend the interests of the workers, we must use union meetings for discussions and put forward demands to them, and must elect to factory councils people who will realise demands.

D. A condition for our actions to be something more than *ad hoc* and haphazard is the existence of a group of workers in a state of constant alertness. This group, even if implicitly at first, can draw up a programme of activity, organise a series of actions, form public opinion, and, in time, come out into the open as independent workers' committees.

E. Wherever there exist strong organised communities of workers who are able to defend their representatives against dismissal from work and imprisonment, free trade union committees should be set up. The experience of employees in the Western democracies shows that this is the most effective way of defending the workers' interests.

Only independent trade unions, having support among the workers whom they represent, have any chance of opposing the authorities. Only they will represent a force with which the authorities must reckon and with which they can deal on equal terms.

We, the undersigned, pledge ourselves to work towards the postulates contained in the Charter of Workers' Rights.

We are also setting up an Aid Fund and pledge constant contributions to it. The resources collected in the Fund will be used to assist persons dismissed from work for taking part in independent union activity.

Gdansk: Bodgan Borusewicz (editor of *Robotnik),* Andrzej Bulc, Joanna Duda-Gwiazda, Andrzej Gwiazda, Andrzej Kolodzieg, Zenon Moskal, Alina Pienkowska, Andrzej Skowron, Bernard Wachowicz, Anna Walentynowica, Lech Walesa, Blazej Wyszkowski, Krzysztof Wyszkowski, Jan Zapolnik.

Gizycko: Henryk Wiurgo, Slawomir Karolik, Leszek Lechowicz, Mieczyslaw Malitka.

Gliwice: Andrzej Gordzewski, Andrzej Spyra (editor of *Robotnik).*

Grudziadz: Maksymilian Mozdrzynski, Edmund Zadrozynski (editor of Robotnik).

Katowice: Kazimierz Switon, Jan Switoná.

Krakow: Franciszek Grabczyk (editor of *Robotnik),* Zygmunt Kaleta.

Lazy: Jerzy Grzebieluch.

Lodz: Jadwiga Szczesna, Stanislaw Sarodzki, Jozef Sreniowski (editor of *Robotnik),* Leszek Witkowski.

Myszkow: Jan Lasek, Ireneusz Maliglowka.

Nowa Ruda: Stefan Kowalczyk.

Pabianice: Marek Chwalewski.

Przemysl: Stanislaw Frydlewicz.

Radom: Anna Ostrowska, Ewa Sobol.

Ruda Slaska: Mieczyslaw Kubiczek.

Skawina: Mieczyslaw Majdok.

Szczecin: Danuta Grajek, Andrzej Jakubcewicz, Tadeusz Kocielowicz, Stefan Kozlowski (editor of *Robotnik),* Zdzislaw Podolski, Jan Witkowski, Miroslaw Witkowski.

Tarnow: Waclaw Mojet, Zbigniew Stanuch.

Torun: Miroslawa Sedzikowska, Stanislaw Smigiel.

Walbrzuch: Jacek Pilichowski (editor of *Robotnik).*

Wlodzislaw Slaski: Boleslaw Cygan.

Warsaw: Henryk Bak, Teodor Klincewicz, Mieczyslaw Ksiezczak, Dariusz Kupiecki (editor of *Robotnik),* Jan Litynski (editor of *Robotnik),* Witold Lucywo (editor of *Robotnik),* Wojciech Onyzkiewicz (editor of *Robotnik),* Henryk Wujec (editor of *Robotnik).*

Wroclaw: Krzystof Grzelczyk, Jacek Malec, Ludwik Werle.

Zabrze: Jacek Wiewiorski.

APPENDIX

Our activities are in accordance with the law. In ratifying the International Labour Pacts and the Conventions of the International Labour Organisation, the government of the Polish People's Republic acknowledged:

I. The right of workers to form associations.

Article 2 from Convention 87 of the International Labour Organisation (Dziennik Ustaw, No. 29, 1958, 125):

Workers and employers, without any discrimination, have the right, without seeking prior permission, to form organisations at their own discretion, and also join such organisations, subject only to adhering to their statutes.

Article 8, point 1a of the International Pact on Economic, Social and Cultural Rights (Appendix of *Dziennik Ustaw*, No. 38, 1977, 169):

'The states party to the present pact pledge themselves to ensure the right to everyone to form and join trade unions at their own choice, in order to support and defend their own economic and social interests, subject only to the condition of observing the statutory regulations of the said organisation. Availing oneself of this right must not be subject to any restrictions other than those provided for in the laws and ordinances of a democratic society in the interests of State security or public order or to protect the rights and freedoms of others.'

II. The right to strike

Article 8 point 1d of the International Pact on Economic, Social and Cultural Rights:

'The states party to the present pact pledge themselves to ensure the right to strike provided that the strike be carried out in accordance with the constitution of the said country.'

APPENDIX 2

The first hours of the strike in the Lenin Shipyard in Gdansk

(This account is taken from the Solidarity strike bulletin that appeared during the Gdansk strike. Issue No. 11 is dated 30th August 1980.

HOW THE STRIKE BEGAN

Our reporter carried out a number of interviews with workers at the shipyards regarding the question of the beginning of the strike. Enclosed are two of them.

First Interview

How did the strike begin?

We agreed with Bogdan that on August 14th we would arrive at work an hour early. We wanted to hang up a number of posters in the cloakrooms about the sacking of Anna Walentynowicz and demanding a wage increase of 1000 zlotys, together with a cost of living supplement. The posters with this information were made by the Movement of Young Poland. In total we had seven of them. I arrived first. Kazik arrived a little while later, with whom I had arranged the day before. Kazik works in Department W3. We went there first of all, where we hung the posters under the clocking-in clock, following which Kazik and a number of his mates stood around guarding the poster, so that no one would tear it down. In the meantime I went back to my department, where I waited for Bogdan. Because he was late I decided to begin on my own. I pasted up the posters and hung them on the doors of a cloakroom, and then went into other cloakrooms where I also hung them. While I was hanging the posters people started congratulating me.

Did the people feel that there was likely to be a strike?
No, but previously we'd informed a small group of trusted people. But in the morning there was talk in the shipyards of a strike.

How did the people take this?
Very well. They asked us detailed questions. Small groups of people started to form meetings with the foremen. I started to inform them that the strike had begun in the whole shipyard and we were meeting outside in the square.

Did the foremen see the posters?
Yes, clearly. Everybody could see them. Even the management.

Did the management attempt to act against them in some way?
No, because around the posters groups of workers stood around, so management was frightened to intervene. Despite that, the first fifteen minutes were rather tense. The foremen did attempt to intervene. So I went to one of the brigades where I knew some of the people and started to explain what we were fighting about. The majority agreed with me. At the request of the foremen, who had started to feel that something was about to happen, we moved away and started to group by the cloakroom. Soon a group of around 30 people formed up, with a similar sized group next to it, by the cloakroom. Fearing that this group might disperse, I went up to them and started to explain about the strike. I explained that the whole shipyard was beginning the strike and that the question was an increase in pay and the matter of Mrs Walentynowicz, who had been thrown out of work unjustly. As I talked, people began to gain in self-confidence.

'Let's go', I said to them. Then a group of around fifty people moved out. We made a banner and just then the director, Barc, arrived and asked what the hell was going on. 'Director', I replied, 'we're on strike.' 'Why strike? Why? What's going on?' To which I replied, 'Can't you read?' and showed him the poster. I left him with a number of workers who had a declaration on the question of Anna. I went off trying to group other people. When I returned, the Party Secretary of the department, Mazurkiewicz, had arrived and was attempting to take away the banner. But the lads were quicker than him and prevented him. The Secretary shouted, 'What's the meaning of this?' to which they replied 'None of your business'. Somebody shoved a number of leaflets into his hand, and everybody surrounded him and started to laugh, because it looked as if the

Party Secretary was handing out leaflets. But I shouted at them to take them away because I didn't want the leaflets to be found in such unworthy hands. When the Secretary left I picked up the banner and led the lads outside into the square. All this had occurred on the terrain of our department.

People were sitting around the square. Suddenly the Deputy Director of the department, Bryczkowski, arrived. This mobilised people. They stood up and started to mill around in the centre of the square. Others joined them. When a large group had been formed a signal was given from a crane. It was a small siren put on for a joke. The Director started to get angry. 'What's going on? Go back to work!' he shouted. But nobody wanted to listen to him. Somebody shouted, 'Have a look at the banner and then you will know what is going on!' A locomotive arrived. It stopped beside us and the driver started to clap. With those formed up on the square, we moved towards the hall of the prefabrication department. We waited there for about five minutes, when suddenly, George and his group arrived. More and more people started to leave the hall. After a while the foremen arrived and started to push people back inside; but the whole of the hall had stopped work. People had left their hammers and were putting away their tools and joining us.

Second interview

How did the strike begin?

I arrived at the shipyards at 4.15. Up until the day of the strike I hadn't told anybody that it was due to begin. In my department there was a majority of Party members and I was worried in case somebody informed the authorities and the strike would fail. I waited, therefore, till the last moment. On the day of the strike I arranged to meet Ludwig. I was the only one from the department. I hung up seven posters and gave five to Ludwig. After doing that I arranged the leaflets, of which I had about 500, and gave one to everybody who entered, saying, 'Take one and read it. Today the whole shipyard is striking'.

Did the leaflet mention that today there was going to be strike?

No, but I had asked the people I trusted the day before what they would do in the event of a strike. Many of them indicated that they would strike, and it was to those people I gave the leaflets, saying, 'Hand them out to other people'. At 5.45 the group formed up by the cloakrooms, about 30 people. Some of them were worried and started saying that the strike would fail. 'Why doesn't a larger department begin the strike?' to which I replied that departments K3 and K4 were already on strike. Then someone said, 'We're not standing here any longer. Let's go back to the hall.' I tried to stop this, but couldn't on my own. But I was aware that if they were to return to the hall where the foremen stood, where the First Secretary and member of the Central Committee, Jan Labedzki, was, everything could fail. People started to return to the machines and turn them on. I went up to them saying, 'Let's go to K3 and K4. They've both stopped'. It was a shot in the dark, because I wasn't certain that anything had happened yet ... but I only wanted to get them to follow me.

At last the workers decided 'OK, let's go!' But even though they stopped the machines, they still hesitated. Finally, the urge to get out won the day.

Thirty or so people gathered together and we left. I took the posters with me. We reached the canteen and then continued on our way throughout the shipyard. Everywhere people were coming out to see what was happening. We shouted to them: 'Leave your machines and come with us!' A good number did join us, and our now rather large group crossed the bridge. People were coming off the ships. They had already stopped work, and yet they hesitated to join us. 'We're not working', they said, 'but we can't join you yet.' It was obvious that they were afraid. We reached department K3, and there we saw a group of people gathered together. This boosted our morale: we were already sure of success, and shouted: 'Hurrah! Hurrah!' People working in the construction offices looked at us through the windows. A crowd was gathered outside, and we went with it to department K3.

A crowd? That's what, about 100 people?

Oh yes! I wanted someone to speak to the people. That would have fired them more, but we weren't in a hurry. We arrived with our banner at the far end of the shipyard, where the director, Wojcik, was already waiting. His first words were: 'What does this mean?' I answered: 'It's a strike!' 'What's it all about?' I said, 'The sacking of Anna Walentynowicz.' 'Anna Walentynowicz?' the director asked. 'You know who she is? She was sacked without notice. Someone like her: she has three order of merit decorations, one in bronze, one in silver and one in gold. She's got thirty years' work behind her, and she's only got five months before she retires.' The director started to move back. Bogdan said to him, 'We won't talk to you for the moment, sir.' We went on and left the director in the crowd. We put our men on the bridge to see that the road was not cut. A lot of people joined our demonstration. We arrived near the gate, where we observed a minute's silence in memory of the victims of 1970. Then we sang the national anthem. Then we went to the excavator, and after we climbed up it was immediately surrounded by the crowd. We gave a speech.

'We have to elect a strike committee. We need people we can trust, who have authority in the work brigades. Let them come forward.' Then the director appeared with his retinue. Since the director was beneath the excavator, we helped him to climb up. But when the director started to speak, Leszek Walesa suddenly appeared. The director didn't see him, for he had climbed on to the excavator from behind. Leszek went up to the director and asked him solemnly, 'Do you recognise me? I worked for ten years in the shipyard, and I still consider myself to be a docker. I have been given the trust of all the workers. It is already four years since I have been without a job.' And he continued, 'We shall hold a sit-in strike!'

At these words, loud hurrahs echoed everywhere. Afterwards, we asked that the director's car should bring Mrs Anna Walentynowicz back to the shipyard. The director protested, but we imposed our will and the director's car went off in search of Mrs Anna. As for us, we went off to the local transmitting centre. That is how the strike began.

APPENDIX 3

The Gdansk Agreement
31 August 1980

This protocol was signed on behalf of the strikers by Lech Walesa (President of the MKS), Andrzej Kolodziej and Bogdan Lis (Vice-Presidents), Mr and Mrs L. Badkowski, W. Gruszewski, A. Gwiazda, S. Izdebski, J. Kmiecik, Z. Kobylinski, H. Krzywonos, S. Lewandowski, A. Pienkowska, Z. Pzybylski, J. Sikorski, L. Sobieszek, T. Stanny, A. Walentynowicz and F. Wisniewski.

It was signed for the governmental commission by: President Mieczyslaw Jagielski (Vice-Prime Minister); M. Zielinski, member of the Secretariat of the Central Committee of the PUWP; T. Fiszbach, President of the Party Committee of Gdansk Voivod and the Mayor of Gdansk, J. Kolodziesk.

The governmental commission and the Inter-Factory Strike Committee (MKS), after studying the twenty-one demands of the workers of the coast who are on strike, have reached the following conclusions:

On Point No. 1 which reads:

"To accept trade unions as free and independent of the Party, as laid down in Convention No. 87 of the ILO and ratified by Poland, which refers to the matter of trade unions rights", **the following decision has been reached:**

1. The activity of the trade union of People's Poland has not lived up to the hopes and aspirations of the workers. We thus consider that it will be beneficial to create new union organisations, which will run themselves, and which will be authentic expressions of the working class. Workers will continue to have the right to join the old trade unions and we are looking at the possibility of the two union structures co-operating.

2. The MKS declares that it will respect the principles laid down in the Polish Constitution while creating the new independent and self-governing unions. These new unions are intended to defend the social and material interests of the workers, and not to play the role of a political party. They will be established on the basis of the socialisation of the means of production and of the socialist system which exists in Poland today. They will recognise the leading role of the PUWP in the State, and will not oppose the existing system of international alliances. Their aim is to ensure for the workers the necessary means for the determination, expression and defence of their interests. The governmental commission will guarantee full respect for the dependence and self-governing character of the new unions in their organisational structures and their functioning at all levels. The govern-

ment will ensure that the new unions have every possibility of carrying out their function of defending the interests of the workers and of seeking the satisfaction of their material, social and cultural needs. Equally it will guarantee that the new unions are not the objects of any discrimination.

3. The creation and the functioning of free and self-governing trade unions is in line with Convention 87 of the ILO relating to trade unions rights and Convention 98, relating to the rights of free association and collective negotiation, both of which conventions have been ratified by Poland. The coming into being of more than one trade union organisation requires changes in the law. The government, therefore, will make the necessary legal changes as regards trade unions, workers' councils and the labour code.

4. The strike committees must be able to turn themselves into institutions representing the workers at the level of the enterprise, whether in the fashion of workers' councils or as preparatory committees of the new trade unions. As a preparatory committee, the MKS is free to adopt the form of a trade union, or of an association of the coastal region. The preparatory committees will remain in existence until the new trade unions are able to organise proper elections to leading bodies. The government undertakes to create the conditions necessary for the recognition of unions outside of the existing Central Council of Trade Unions.

5. The new trade unions should be able to participate in decisions affecting the conditions of the workers in such matters as the division of the national assets between consumption and accumulation, the division of the social consumption fund (health, education, culture), the wages policy, in particular with regard to an automatic increase of wages in line with inflation, the economic plan, the direction of investment and prices policy. The government undertakes to ensure the conditions necessary for the carrying out of these functions.

6. The enterprise committee will set up a research centre whose aim will be to engage in an objective analysis of the situation of the workers and employees, and will attempt to determine the correct ways in which their interests can be represented. This centre will also provide the information and expertise necessary for dealing with such questions as the prices index and wages index and the forms of compensation required to deal with price rises. The new unions should have their own publications.

7. The government will enforce respect for Article 1 of the trade union law of 1949, which guarantees the workers the right to freely come together to form trade unions. The new trade union will not join the Central Council of Trade unions (CRZZ). It is agreed that the new trade union law will respect these principles. The participation of members of the MKS and of the preparatory committees for the new trade unions in the elaboration of the new legislation is also guaranteed.

On Point No. 2 which reads;
"To guarantee the right to strike, and the security of strikers and those who help them", **it has been agreed that:**
The right to strike will be guaranteed by the new trade union law. The law will have to define the circumstances in which strikes can be called and organised, the ways in which conflicts can be resolved, and the penalties for

infringements of the law. Articles 52, 64 and 65 of the labour code (which outlaw strikes) will cease to have effect from now until the new law comes into practice. The government undertakes to protect the personal security of strikers and those who have helped them and to ensure against any deterioration in their conditions of work.

With regard to Point No. 3 which reads:
"To respect freedom of expression and publication, as upheld by the Constitution of People's Poland, and to take no measures against independent publications, as well as to grant access to the mass media to representatives of all religions", **it has been added that:**
1. The government will bring before the Sejm (Parliament) within three months a proposal for a law on control of the press, of publications, and of other public manifestations, which will be based on the following principles: censorship must protect the interests of the State. This means the protection of State secrets, and of economic secrets in the sense that these will be defined in the new legislation, the protection of State interests and its international interests, the protection of religious convictions, as well as the right of non-believers, as well as the suppression of publications which offend against morality.

The proposals will include the right to make a complaint against the press control and similar institutions to a higher administrative tribunal. This law will be incorporated in an amendment to the administrative code.
2. The access to the mass media by religious organisations in the course of their religious activities will be worked out through an agreement between the State institutions and the religious associations on matters of content and of organisation. The government will ensure the transmission by radio of the Sunday Mass through a specific agreement with the Church hierarchy.
3. The radio and television as well as the press and publishing houses must offer expression to different points of view. They must be under the control of society.
4. The press, as well as citizens and their organisations, must have access to public documents, and above all to administrative instructions and socioeconomic plans, in the form in which they are published by the government and by the administrative bodies which draw them up. Exceptions to the principle of open administration will be legally defined in agreement with Point No. 3 para 1.

With regard to Point No. 4, which reads:
"To re-establish the rights of people who were sacked after the strikes in 1970 and 1976 and of students who have been excluded from institutions of higher education because of their opinions, (b) to free all political prisoners, including Edmund Zadrozynski, Jan Kozlowski and Marek Kozlowski; (c) to cease repression against people for their opinions", **it has been agreed:**
(a) to immediately investigate the reasons given for the sackings after the strikes of 1970 and 1976. In every case where injustice is revealed, the person involved must be re-instated, taking into account any new qualifications that person may have acquired. The same principle will be applied in the case of students.

(b) the cases of persons mentioned under point (b) should be put to the Ministry of Justice, which within two weeks will study their dossiers. In cases where those mentioned are already imprisoned, they must be released pending this investigation, and until a new decision on their case is reached.
(c) to launch an immediate investigation into the reasons for the arrests of those mentioned (the three named individuals).
(d) to institute full liberty of expression in public and professional life.

On Point No. 5, which reads:
"To inform the public about the creation of the MKS and its demands, through the mass media", **it has been decided that:**
This demand shall be met through the publication in all national mass media of the full text of this agreement.

On Point No. 6, which reads:
"To implement the measures necessary for resolving the crisis, starting with the publication of all the relevant information on the socio-economic situation, and to allow all groups to participate in a discussion on a programme of economic reforms", **the following has been agreed:**

We consider it essential to speed up the preparation of an economic reform. The authorities will work out and publish the basic principles of such a reform in the next few months. It is necessary to allow for wider participation in a public discussion of the reform. In particular the trade unions must take part in the working out of laws relating to the enterprises and to workers' self-management. The economic reform must be based on the strengthening, autonomous operation and participation of the workers' councils in management. Specific regulations will be drawn up in order to guarantee that the trade unions will be able to carry out their functions as set out in Point No. 1 of this agreement.

Only a society which has a firm grasp of reality can take the initiative in reforming the economy. The government will significantly increase the areas of socio-economic information to which society, the trade unions and other social and economic organisations have access.

The MKS also suggests, in order that a proper perspective be provided for the development of the family agricultural units, which are the basis of Polish agriculture, that the individual and collective sectors of agriculture should have equal access to the means of production, including the land itself, and that the conditions should be created for the recreation of self-governing co-operatives.

On Point No. 7, which reads:
"To pay all the workers who have taken part in the strike for the period of the strike as if they were on paid holiday throughout this period, with payment to be made from the funds of the CRZZ", **the following decision has been reached:**

Workers and employers participating in the strike will receive, on their return to work, 40 per cent of their wages. The rest, which will add up to a full 100 per cent of the nominal basic wage, will be calulated as would holiday pay, on the basis of an 8-hour working day. The MKS calls on workers who are members to work towards the increase of output, to improve the use of materials and energy, and to show greater work discipline, when the strike is over, and to do this in co-operation with the management of the factories and enterprises.

On Point No. 8, which reads:
"To increase the minimum wage for every worker by 2000 zlotys a month to compensate for the increase in prices", **the following has been decided:**
These wage increases will be introduced gradually, and will apply to all types of workers and employees and in particular to those who receive the lowest wages. The increases will be worked out through agreements in individual factories and branches. The implementation of the increases will take into account the specific character of particular professions and sectors. The intention will be to increase wages through revising the wage scale or through increasing other elements of the wage.

White-collar workers in the enterprises will receive salary increases on an individual basis. These increases will be put into effect between now and the end of September 1980, on the basis of the agreement reached in each branch.

After reviewing the situation in all the branches, the government will present, by 31st October 1980, in agreement with the trade unions, a programme of pay increases to come into effect from 1st January 1981 for those who get the least at the moment, paying particular attention to large families.

On Point No. 9, which reads:
"To guarantee the sliding scale", **the following decision has been reached:**
It is necessary to slow down the rate of inflation through stricter control over both the public and private sectors, and in particular through the suppression of hidden prices increases.

Following on from a government decision, investigation will be carried out into the cost of living. These studies will be carried out both by the trade unions and by scientific institutions. By the end of 1980, the government will set out the principles of a system of compensation for inflation, and these principles will be open to discussion by the public. When they have been accepted, they will come into effect. It will be necessary to deal with the question of the social minimum in elaborating these principles.

On Point No. 10, which reads:
"To ensure the supply of products on the internal market, and to export only the surplus",

and Point No. 11, which reads:
"to suppress commercial prices and the use of foreign currency in sales on the internal market",

and Point No. 12, which reads:
"To introduce ration cards for meat and meat-based products, until the market situation can be brought under control",
the following agreement has been reached:

The supply of meat will be improved between now and 31st December 1980, through an increase in the profitability of agricultural production and the limitation of the export of meat to what is absolutely indispensable, as well as through the import of extra meat supplies. At the same time, during this period a programme for the improvement of the meat supply will be drawn up, which will take into account the possibility of the introduction of a rationing system through the issue of cards.

Products which are scarce on the national market for current consumption will not be sold in the 'Pewex' shops; and between now and the end of the year, the population will be informed of all decisions which are taken concerning the problems of supply.

The MKS has called for the abolition of the special shops and the levelling out of the price of meat and related products.

On Point No. 13, which reads:
"To introduce the principle of cadre selection on the basis of qualitications, not on the basis of membership of the party, and to abolish the privileges of the police (MO) and the security services (SB), and of the Party apparatus, through the abolition of special sources of supply, through the equalisation of family allowances, etc." **we have reached the following agreement:**

The demand for cadres to be selected on the basis of qualifications and ability has been accepted. Cadres can be members of the PUWP, of the SD (the Democratic Party, which draws its membership from small private enterprises), of the ZSL (the Peasant Party — these three parties make up the National Front) or of no party. A programme for the equalisation of the family allowances of all the professional groups will be presented by the government before 31st December 1980. The governmental commission states that only employees' restaurants and canteens, such as those in other work establishments and offices, are operated.

On Point 14, which reads:
"To allow workers to retire at 50 years for women and 55 for men, or after 30 years of work for women, and 35 years for men, regardless of age", **it has been agreed that:**
The governmental commission declares pensions will be increased each year, taking into account the real economic possibilities and the rise in the lowest wages. Between now and 1st December 1981, the government will work out and present a programme on these questions. The government will work out plans for the increase of old age and other pensions up to the social minimum as established through studies carried out by scientific institutions; these will be presented to the public and submitted to the control of the trade unions.

The MKS stresses the great urgency of these matters and will continue to raise the demands for the increase of old age and other pensions, taking into account the increase of the cost of living.

On Point No. 15, which reads:
"To increase the old-style pensions to the level paid under the new system", **it has been agreed:**
The governmental commission states that the lowest pensions will be increased every year as a function of rises in the lowest wages. The government will present a programme to this effect between now and 1st December 1981. The government will draft proposals for a rise in the lowest pensions to the level of the social minimum as defined in studies

made by scientific institutes. These proposals will be presented to the public and subject to control by the unions.

On Point No. 16, which reads:
"To improve working conditions and the health services so as to ensure better medical protection for the workers", **it has been agreed that:**
It is necessary to increase immediately the resources put into the sphere of the health services, to improve medical supplies through the import of basic materials where these are lacking, to increase the salaries of all health workers, and with the utmost urgency on the part of the government and the ministries, to prepare programmes for improving the health of the population. Other measures to be taken in this area are put foward in the appendix.

Addendum to Point 16:
1. To introduce a "Charter of Rights for Health Service Employees".
2. To guarantee supplies for sale of an adequate amount of protective cotton clothing.
3. To refund health service workers for the purchase of work clothes from the material expenditure fund.
4. To provide a guaranteed wage fund that would make possible rewarding all those who have performed outstanding work in accordance with the theoretically existing possibilities.
5. To set up funds for additional payments upon the completion of 25 and 30 years of work.
6. To establish additional payment for work under difficult or harmful working conditions, and to introduce additional pay for shift work by non-medical employees.
7. To restore additional payment to those attending patients with infectious diseases or to those handling contagious biological material and to increase pay for nurses on night duty.
8. To recognise spinal diseases as occupational for dentists.
9. Allocation of good quality fuel to hospitals and nurseries.
10. To recognise additional payment for years of service to nurses without secondary school diplomas, to bring them up to the earnings level of graduate nurses.
11. To introduce a seven-hour work day for all skilled workers.
12. To introduce free Saturdays without the requirement of making up the time otherwise.
13. Sunday and holiday duties to be paid by a 100 per cent increase in wages.
14. Making medicine available free of charge to health service workers.
15. Making it possible to make a partial refund of housing loans from the social fund.
16. To increase the allocated apartment space for health service workers.
17. To make it easier for nurses living alone to be allotted apartments.
18. To change the award fund into a 13th monthly salary.
19. To give a six-week vacation to health service workers after 20 years of service and to make it possible for them to receive an annual paid vacation for health reasons, as is enjoyed by teachers.

20. To give people working for their M.D's four-week vacations and those working for specialised degrees two-week vacations.
21. To guarantee a doctor the right to a day off after night duty.
22. To give workers in nurseries and kindergartens a five-hour schedule, as well as free board.
23. To introduce allocation of cars for basic health service workers and a mileage limit or a lump sum refund for business travel.
24. Nurses with higher education should be recognised and paid the same as other workers with a higher education.
25. To create specially trained repair groups in the ZOZs (factory health centres) to protect health service buildings from further deterioration.
26. To increase the per capita standard allowance for medicines for hospital patients from 1,138 loty to 2,700 zloty, since the latter is the actual cost of treatment, and to increase the nutrition allowance as well.
27. To set up a system of food vouchers for the bedridden.
28. To double the number of ambulances — this being a real need today.
29. To take steps to guarantee purity of air, soil and water, especially coastal seawater.
30. Along with being provided with new housing developments, citizens must also be provided with health centres, drug-stores and nurseries.

On Point No. 17, which reads:
"To ensure sufficient places in creches and play schools for the children of all working women", **it has been agreed that:**

The government commission is fully in agreement with this demand. The provincial authorities will present proposals on this question before 30th November 1980.

On Point No. 18, which reads:
"To increase the length of maternity leave to three years to allow a mother to bring up her child", **is has been decided that:**

Before 31st December 1980, an analysis of the possibilities open to the national economy will be made in consultation with the trade unions, on the basis of which an increase in the monthly allowance for women who are on unpaid maternity leave will be worked out.

The MKS asks that this analysis should include an allowance which will provide 100 per cent of pay for the first year after birth, and 50 per cent for the second year, with a fixed minimum of 2,000 zlotys a month. This goal should be gradually reached from the first half of 1981 onwards.

On Point No. 19, which reads:
"To reduce the waiting period for the allocation of housing", **the following agreement has been reached:**

The district authorities will present a programme of measures for improving the accommodation situation and for reducing the waiting list for receipt of accommodation, before 31st December 1980. These proposals will be put forward for a wide-ranging discussion in the district, and competent organisations, such as the Polish Town Planners' Association, the Central Association of Technicians etc., will be consulted. The proposals should refer both to ways of using the present building enterprises and prefabricated housing factories, and to a thorough-going development of the industry's productive base. Similar action will be taken throughout the country.

On Point No. 20, which reads:
"To increase the travelling allowance from 40 to 100 zlotys, and to introduce a cost of living bonus", **it has been agreed that:**
An agreement will be reached on the question of raising the travelling allowance and compensation, to take effect from 1st January 1981. The proposals for this to be ready by 31st October 1980.

On Point No. 21, which reads:
"To make Saturday a holiday in factories where there is continuing production, where there is a four-shift system. Saturday working must be compensated for by a commensurate increase in the number of holidays, or through the establishment of another free day in the week", **it has been agreed that:**
The principle that Saturday should be a free day should be put into effect, or another method of providing free time should be devised. This should be worked out by 31st December 1980. The measures should include the increase in the number of free Saturdays from the start of 1981. Other possibilities relating to this point are mentioned in the appendix, or appear in the submissions of the MKS.

Addendum to Point 21:
1. Change the Council of Ministers' decree concerning the method of calculating vacation pay as well as sickness benefits for those working under the four-shift system. At present, an average of 30 days is used (while they work 22 days in a month). This method of calculation decreases the average day's wages during short sick leaves and lowers the vacation equivalent.
2. We demand regularisation, by one legal act (a Council of Ministers' decree), of the principles governing calculation of earnings for periods of absence from work in individual cases. The obscurity of the rules at the moment is used against workers.
3. The lack of Saturdays off for workers on the four-shift system should be compensated for by additional days off. The number of days granted in the four-shift system is higher than anywhere else, but they serve as additional periods of rest after exhausting work, not as real days off. The administration's argument that such compensation should be granted only after the number of working hours in both systems have been made the same does not seem justified.
4. We demand all Saturdays off every month as is the case in other socialist countries.
5. We demand removal of Article 147 from the Labour Code, which permits extending time to 9 hours a day in a week preceding additional days off, as well as Article 148. At the moment, we have one of the longest working weeks in Europe.
6. Upgrade the importance of agreements concerning remuneration by introducing appropriate changes in the Labour Code. These should

specify that both changes in individual salary grading or in other components of pay, and also a change in method of payment (from daily
wage to piece-work) require notification by the employer. One should
also introduce the principle that the system under which individuals are
classified for purposes of setting piece-work rates be made to cover
basically all types of work performed by the worker. It is also necessary
to systematise the ways in which young workers are made use of, in
keeping with their qualifications, so that the above settlement does not
become an additional obstacle to their professional advancement.
7. Employees working night shift should be granted up to a 50 per cent
   supplement if under the daily wage system and 30 per cent more real pay
   if under the piece-work system.

After reaching the above agreement, it has also been decided that:
The government undertakes:
to ensure personal security and to allow both those who have taken part in
the strike and those who have supported it to return to their previous
work under the previous conditions;
to take up at the ministerial level the specific demands raised by the workers
of all enterprises represented in the MKS;
to publish immediately the complete text of this agreement in the press, the
radio, the television, and in the national mass media.
The strike committee undertakes to propose the ending of the strike from
5.00pm on 31st August 1980.

APPENDIX 4

*Text of a speech by Lech Walesa at International Labour Conference,
Geneva, 5th June 1981.*

I have come to this Conference as a delegate of Polish workers, accompanied by my colleagues from the Solidarity trade union and colleagues
from the two other trade union federations in Poland, the branch unions
and the autonomous unions.

This is clear proof of the pluralism of the Polish trade union movement.
However, I have taken the floor here, first of all, as a representative of the
largest Polish trade union organisation, the independent, self-managed
trade union Solidarity.

This organisation was born late in August 1980 as a result of the
memorable events in the shipyards of Gdańsk, Gdynia and Szczecin and in
the coalmines of Silesia.

In just a few months, we have brought together in our ranks millions of
workers in every sphere of the national economy and Solidarity has become
the largest social organisation in the history of my country. Its members
have different levels of education, different occupations and vocations, different philosophical and religious opinions, but they are joined by one
common aspiration, that of ensuring for the Polish workers, blue-collar
and white-collar alike, a life in civic freedom, freedom of thought and
speech, human dignity and national sovereignty.

We all hoped that Pope John Paul II would honour this Conference with his presence, but this hope was frustrated by the criminal attack on his life. I should like to refer here to some of the Pope's thoughts.

At a meeting with the delegation of Solidarity in Rome, Pope John Paul II described the Gdańsk Agreement and the birth of our union in the following way: "Against the background of events which are so numerous in this world of ours and in which violence and brutal force prevail only too often as a method of action, against the background of terrorism in so many countries which does not spare the lives of innocent people, this way of acting without violence and without force, this way of seeking solutions through a thoughtful dialogue that takes into account the common good, is a tribute both to the representatives of the working people from the Baltic coast, from Silesia and from other regions, who now belong to Solidarity, and to the representatives of the Polish Government".

These words are for us an important message whose significance goes beyond the limits of one country only.

The independence of our union, which has brought about a new social situation in my country, sometimes gives rise to various fears and comments.

I should like, from this international forum, to tell everybody, all the peoples and all the countries in the world, that the Poles are capable of settling their own internal affairs among themselves and by themselves. It is in the common interest that no external intervention should prevent the process of consolidation of the Polish society which began on 31 August 1980.

Our union was born out of protest. Using the traditional methods of workers' struggle — demonstrations and strikes — it contributed in a definitive way to initiating a thoroughgoing transformation of the social and political life of the country. There is no area which has remained unaffected by this process of renewal. And even though we are aware that this is only the beginning of these changes, no-one in Poland has any doubt that there is no way to return to the old methods of ruling the country and governing its economy.

The Director-General's Report mentions the circumstances in which our union was registered. I should like to add to the information given there that, in recent weeks, a further step was taken towards creating new trade unions in Poland. On 12 May an independent trade union of individual peasants, Solidarity, was registered whose membership consists of several million peasant owners of small family farms. Thus a cornerstone has been placed under a true alliance of workers and peasants, under the lasting co-operation of all the working people in Poland.

The whole world knows what a difficult economic situation my country is in as a result of the political errors and the irresponsible economic and social policies pursued by the leaders of my country in past years. Overcoming this deep crisis is not a matter of weeks or months. The independent, self-managed trade union Solidarity has declared its readiness to co-operate in implementing any rational programme aimed at overcoming the crisis and reforming the existing structures of the social and economic life of our country. We are conscious of the fact that to find a way out of the present difficulties will require sacrifices and self-denial on the part of every

Pole, even though he bears no responsibility whatever for our economic collapse. We have recommended every section of Solidarity not to make any wage demands and not to go on strike without the agreement of the leadership of Solidarity. But we shall continue our struggle so that no-one in Poland remains jobless and so that the vital interests of the most deprived segments of the population in town and country are well protected.

Our trade union attaches great importance to setting up, in accordance with the traditions of our workers' councils set up in 1956, a genuine system of workers' self-management of socialist-inspired enterprises, in conjunction with a fundamental change in the methods of managing the national economy. The self-management bodies and all the trade union sections will be faced with the arduous task of improving rapidly the protection of the employment and health of our workers, where there is still much room for improvement.

May I emphasise that Polish workers belonging to the independent, self-managed trade union Solidarity greatly appreciate the possibility of co-operating with the ILO and are ready to participate actively in the formulation and development of international labour laws and other ways of bringing about social progress on a world scale.

It is a matter of personal privilege and honour to me to be able to participate in the present session of the ILO Conference and to be able to meet and co-operate with so many trade unionists from all the countries of the world.

Polish trade unionists have co-operated with the ILO wholeheartedly throughout the 62 years of its existence. When in August 1980 we decided to create independent, self-managed trade unions, we used in full the provisions of the ILO Conventions Nos.87 and 98 on freedom of association and trade union rights to strengthen Solidarity. I hope that in the future, too, our co-operation with the ILO will be a lasting element in the mutual relations of Polish trade unionists with trade unions from all over the world and with international organisations working for social progress and social justice.

I should like to express our solidarity with working people throughout the world, with the struggle waged by trade union organisations in defence of the social interests of the working people, in defence of dignity of work, for the protection of human rights wherever they are being infringed. A man of our times cannot have a clear conscience so long as there are areas in the world where poverty and famine prevail, so long as heart-rending contrast in material and social well-being exist between different countries or classes of people, so long as man's natural pursuit of freedom, a decent life and happiness are countered by violence, oppression and exploitation.

May I express the hope that — irrespective of any dividing line between States, blocs or systems — the principles of social justice, democratic freedom and independence of the trade union movement, which are the guidelines of Solidarity, may be the common property and underlying force of the entire trade union movement.

APPENDIX 5

The Nomenklatura

This list was first published in France in *Revue Francaise de Sociologie,* number 2, April-June 1979. The list comes from three directives of the Central Committee of the Polish Communist Party dating from 1972. We are grateful to *Labour Focus on Eastern Europe* for permission to use their translation of the text.

Lists of posts falling under the *nomenklatura* of the Party Central Committee, regional committees and district (town and neighbourhood) committees.

A. Nomenklatura posts of the Party Central Committee

I. Party functions: personnel politically responsible for Party bodies and publications; secretaries of Party committees

1. Heads of Central Committee departments, their deputies, the inspectors, main instructors and political reporters of the Central Committee.
2. The first secretaries and zonal secretaries of regional Party committees.
3. The rector, vice-rectors, institute (group) directors, and scientific workers at the Academy of Social Sciences.
4. The chief and deputy editors of *Trybuna Ludu, Nowe Drogi, Zycie Parti* and *Chlopska Droga.*
5. The directors of the Bydgoszcz and Katowice Party schools.
6. The first secretaries of Party committees in the ministries and central state administration.

II. High state functions: the administration of state and economy

1. The president and vice-presidents of the Diet of the People's Republic of Poland.
2. The president and deputy-presidents, the secretary and members of the Council of State.
3. The president and vice-presidents of the Council of Ministers.
4. The president and vice-presidents of the Supreme Chamber of Control.
5. The president and vice-presidents of the Council of Ministers Planning Commission.
6. Ministers, vice-ministers and directors-general.
7. Chairmen of the presidia of regional people's councils.
8. Ambassadors and plenipotentiaries, embassy and legation advisors, consuls-general.
9. The presidents of the Supreme Court and regional tribunals.
10. The public prosecutor of the People's Republic of Poland, his deputies, and regional public prosecutors.
11. The president and vice-presidents of the Polish Academy of Sciences, the administrative secretary and his assistants.

12. The head of the Diet Chancellory and the Council of State Chancellory.
13. The commander-in-chief of the police force, and his deputy.
14. Regional commanders, their first deputies charged with state security, the first deputies charged with the police.
15. The chairman and vice-chairmen of the National Raw Materials Board.
16. The chairman of the National Mining Board.
17. The presidents and vice-presidents of the State Administration.
18. The president and vice-presidents of the National Bank of Poland, and the directors of central banks.
19. Delegates of the government of the People's Republic of Poland.
20. The chairmen and vice-chairmen of the central, regional and sectional boards of the Co-operative Unions.
21. Members of the secretariat of artisan organisations.
22. The directors-general of nationwide industrial unions and of the central management and offices of domestic trade.
23. The regional directors-general of the Polish Railways and of National Telecommunications.
24. The directors-general of the regional unions of Public Works.
25. The commander-in-chief of the Fire Brigade.
26. The directors-general of public institutions (Lot, Orbis, Wars. etc.).
27. The deputy to the permanent Comecon representative of the People's Republic of Poland, the deputy to the Comecon secretary-general nominated by the People's Republic of Poland.
28. Directors of the various Polish offices abroad; the departmental heads of the Comecon Secretariat and UN Secretariat nominated by the People's Republic of Poland.

III. Functions in social organisations

1. The president, vice-president and secretary of the Polish Committee of the National Unity Front.
2. The presidents, vice-presidents and secretaries of the Central Trade Union Council; the presidents, vice-presidents and secretaries of the Trade Union Federations.
3. The president, secretary-general and secretaries of the Association of Fighters for Freedom and Democracy.
4. The presidents, vice-presidents and secretaries of the youth organisations.
5. The president of the National Women's Council, and the president of the League of Women.
6. The presidents and secretaries-general of the Higher Technical Organisation and the Polish Economic Society.
7. The chairman of the Higher Council of Cooperatives.
8. The president, *ex officio* vice-presidents and secretaries of the Polish-Soviet Friendship Association.
9. The president and secretary-general of the Society of Polish Journalists.
10. The president and secretary-general of the Union of Polish Writers.

11. The president and secretary-general of the Association of Polish Jurists.
12. The president of the Higher Lawyers Council.
13. The president and vice-presidents of the Union of Agricultural Circles.
14. The president and vice-presidents of the Union of Agricultural Producer Co-operatives.
15. Full-time presidents, vice-presidents and secretaries of social and cultural associations.
16. The president of the National Defence League.
17. The president and vice-presidents of the Volunteer Firemens Association.

IV. Functions in the Army

1. The head and deputy-head of the General Staff.
2. The head and deputy-heads of the political directorate of the Army.
3. The inspector-general of Home Defence.
4. The inspector-general of (military) instruction.
5. The Senior Commissariat officer.
6. The inspector-general of the Engineering Corps.
7. The commanders of military regions and their assistants responsible for political matters.
8. Commanders of the Armed Forces and their deputies responsible for political matters in: (a) the air force, (b) the navy, (c) aerial defence, and (d) military defence of the frontiers.
9. The head of the Internal Military Corps.
10. The head of the personnel department at the Ministry of National Defence.
11. The head of the (Military) Instruction Inspectorate.
12. The head of the Home Defence Inspectorate.
13. The head of the directorate of the Second General Staff.
14. Persons proposed for the rank of general.

V. Functions in the mass media, publishing houses and scientific institutions

1. The chairman, deputies and directors-general of the Radio and Television Board.
2. The chairman, vice-chairmen and directors of the 'RSW-Prasa' Board.
3. The chief and deputy editors and the directors of the Polish Press Agency, the Polish 'Interpress' Agency, the Central Photographic Agency, Artistic and Graphic Publications, the Society for Documentary Film Production, and Polish Film News.
4. The director of the publishing co-operative *Ksiazka i Wiedza*.
5. The chief editors of *Ideologia i Polityka* and *Zagadnienia i Materialy*.
6. The directors and chief editors of scientific and literary publishing houses.
7. The chief editors of national circulation dailies, weeklies and monthlies.
8. The directors-general of Polish Radio and Television.

9. The directors of specialised national institutes of scientific research.
10. The directors of the foreign broadcasting service of the Polish Academy of Sciences.
11. Departmental secretaries and assistant secretaries, as well as directors of the Bureau of the Polish Academy of Sciences.

B. Nomenklatura posts of regional Party committees

I. Party functions: personnel politically responsible for Party bodies and publications; the secretaries of Party committees

1. The first secretary and the secretaries of various sections of the district, town and neighbourhood committees.
2. Personnel politically responsible for the regional Party committees.
3. The chief and deputy editors and the secretaries of the regional committee press.
4. The first secretaries of Party committees in higher education; the first secretary of Party committees in the presidia of regional people's councils; the first secretary in the regional police directorate.
5. Full-time secretaries of Party committees in enterprises and combines falling under the regional committee *nomenklatura*, including all those placed under Central Committee management.

II. Functions in government bodies, regional administration and the economic apparatus

1. The vice-chairmen and secretaries of the presidia of regional people's councils.
2. The chairman of the Regional Economic Planning Commission, and regional school inspectors.
3. Heads of departments of the regional people's council presidia (as estimated by the executive committees of the regional Party committee).
4. Deputy regional commanders (except the first deputies responsible for State Security and for the Police).
5. Heads of departments of the regional police force (as estimated by the executive committees of the regional Party committee).
6. The vice-presidents of regional tribunals.
7. Deputy regional public prosecutors.
8. The directors of regional penal institutions.
9. The chairmen of (regional) delegations to the Supreme Chamber of Control, the regional inspectors of P.I.H. and O.K.R.
10. The presidium chairmen of district, town and neighbourhood people's councils.
11. District police commanders and their deputies responsible for State Security.
12. The presidents of district tribunals.
13. District public prosecutors.

14. The presidents of regional administrative tribunals for social insurance.
15. The chairmen of regional arbitration commissions.
16. The directors (presidents) of regional economic organisations, industry unions, regional organs, and regionally administered co-operatives and enterprises (except the chief director of the regional union of Public Works).
17. Regional branch directors of the National Bank of Poland, the Agricultural Bank, the Polish Savings Bank, the State Insurance House, and the Social Insurance Department.
18. The directors-general of key combines and enterprises (and deputy directors if so decided by the regional Party committee).
19. Regional commanders of the Fire Brigade.
20. Directors of medical establishments and of the social services.
21. Leaders of the regional delegations of the General Office for the Supervision of Press, Publications and Public Performances.

III. Functions in social organisations

1. The presidents, vice-presidents and secretaries of regional committees of the National Unity Front.
2. The presidents, vice-presidents and secretaries of the regional trade-union councils.
3. The presidents, vice-presidents and secretaries of the regional leaderships of youth organisations.
4. The president and (full-time) members of the regional leadership of the Association of Fighters for Freedom and Democracy.
5. The chairmen, vice-chairmen and secretaries of the regional leadership of the Union of Agricultural Circles.
6. The presidents of the regional women's council and of the regional League of Women leadership.
7. The presidents, vice-presidents and secretaries of the regional leadership of the Trade Union Federations.
8. The regional presidents and full-time leaders of artistic, social, cultural, sporting and para-military associations, as well as professional bodies such as the Higher Technical Organisation and the Association of Polish Jurists.

IV. Functions in the mass media, publishing houses and scientific institutions

1. The chief and deputy directors of Polish Radio broadcasting stations and of Polish Television centres.
2. The chief and deputy editors of the main local dailies and cultural and social magazines.
3. The chief and deputy editors of regional press and book publishing houses.
4. The rectors and vice-rectors of higher education establishments.
5. Theatre managers and artistic directors.
6. The directors of (regional) museums.

C. Nomenklatura posts of district (town and neighbourhood) Party committees

I. Functions in the party: personnel politically responsible for Party bodies; secretaries of Party committees

1. Those politically responsible for district (town and neighbourhood) committees.
2. The first secretaries of town committees (not integrated into a district) and of rural communes.
3. The (full-time) secretaries of Party base committees and organisations in enterprises coming under the district *nomenklatura*.

II. Functions in government bodies, local administration and the economic apparatus

1. The vice-presidents and secretaries of the presidia of district, town and neighbourhood people's councils.
2. The chairman of the District Economic Planning Commission, and the departmental heads of the district people's council presidia (as estimated by the executive committee of the district Party committee).
3. Primary and secondary school inspectors, the heads of secondary technical colleges.
4. The vice-presidents of district tribunals.
5. Deputy district public prosecutors.
6. Assistant district police commanders (not coming under the regional Party committee *nomenklatura*).
7. The chairmen of people's councils in towns not integrated into a district.
8. The chairmen of commune people's councils, and commune heads.
9. Commune police station chiefs.
10. District commanders of the Citizens Volunteer Militia.
11. District commanders of the Fire Brigade.
12. The directors of state farms, both integrated and autonomous.
14. The directors (presidents) of district economic organs.
15. Branch directors of the National Bank of Poland, the Agricultural Bank, the Polish Savings Bank, the State Insurance House, S.O.P., at the level of one or more districts.
16. The directors of industrial-commercial enterprises for public workers and the supply of services (not coming under the regional Party committee *nomenklatura*); the chairman of co-operatives.
17. The directors (heads) of important medical establishments (hospitals, sanitoria).
18. The directors of enterprises forming part of a combine; the directors of factories forming part of a multi-factory enterprise.

III. Functions in social organisations

1. The presidents of district committees of the National Unity Front.
2. The presidents of district trade-union commissions.

3. The presidents of the district leaderships of the Associations of Fighters for Freedom and Democracy.
4. The presidents of the district leaderships of youth organisations.
5. The presidents of the district leaderships of Agricultural Circles.
6. The presidents of the district women's council and of the district League of Women leadership.
7. The presidents of district physical culture committees.

Warsaw, October 1972

APPENDIX 6

Making Contact with Solidarity

It is easy enough to get in touch with Solidarity by simply writing to NSZZ "Solidarnosc" followed by the town or city in Poland. Poland's postal service is full of Solidarity members, and letters and parcels generally get through. In the bigger towns and cities Solidarity offices will easily find someone who can read English and translate messages of support from trade unionists outside of Poland. Polish addresses place the city first, followed by the street, so the correct address for Warsaw Solidarity is:

NSZZ "Solidarnosc"
Warsaw 00-031
ul. Mokotowska 16-20
Poland.

It is also easy to dial direct to Poland though obviously there is no guarantee that an English speaker will be at the other end of the line. On the other hand it is easy to send a telex direct to a Solidarity office and, again, in the big offices such as Gdansk, Warsaw, Szczecin, there are English speaking officials who can translate the telex.

Tourist visits to Poland are easy to arrange and the charter flight from London plus obligatory purchase of Polish currency costs around £150. Hotels are very cheap and internal transport in Poland is also cheap. Formal trade union visits should be cleared with the Gdansk headquarters international department but all Solidarity offices will welcome, even at short notice, trade union visitors from outside Poland.

Addresses of Solidarity in Poland

Bialystok
ul. Nowotki 13
tel: 366-55

*Bielsko-Biala/*Beskidy/*43-300*
ul. Boh.W-wy 2/120
tel: 232-72
    287-27
telex: 0562197

Bydgoszcz 85-068
ul. Marchlewskiggos
tel: 220-509

Bytom 41-902
ul. Bieruta 58
tel: 81-14,51
    w. 694
    81-94-29   telex: 033250

Cracow 31-111
ul. Krasinsuicgo 11b
tel: 249-97
telex: 0322701

Czestochowa 42-200
ul. Kościuszki 18/20
tel: 412-21
      478-76
telex: 037248

Elblag 82-300
ul. Lacznosci 3
tel: 7025

Gdańsk 80-244
ul. Grunwaldzka 103
tel: 41-11-11
      41-62-34
      41-95-26
telex: 0512184

Gizycko 11-500
ul. Obroncow Stalingradu 13
tel: 35-45
telex: 0526255

Glogów 67-200
ul. Jedności Robotn. 14
/Huta Miedzi/
tel: 36-683
      34-510
      33-112
telex: 0782668

Gorzów Wlkp. 66-400
ul. Krajowez Raoy Narodowej 31
tel: 272-31
      249-08
telex: 044546

Grudziadz 86-300
ul. Pulaskiego 8a
tel: 269-95
      215-62
      217-75
      276-12
telex: 055212

Jarocin 63-200
ul. PPR 34
tel: 31-61
      w.20

Jaroslaw 37-500
ul. Kraszewskiego 19
/Huta Szkla/
tel: 57-88
telex: 1633468

Jastrzebie Zdrój 44-330
ul. 1-go Maja 23
tel: 620-74
telex: 816077 a

Jelenia Góra 58-500
ul. Kasprowicza 17
tel: 230-04
      231-63
      236-93

Katowice 40-058
Huta Katowice
ul. Stelmacha 17
tel: 519403
      516006
telex: 0315292

Kalisz 62-800
al. Wolnosci 4
tel: 727-44
telex: 0462600

Koszalin 75-640
ul. Zwyciestwa 137-139
tel: 279-21
      w. 151
telex: 0534843

Kutno 99-300
ul. Krolewska 11
tel: 37-02
      21-30
telex: 8400

Krosno 38-400
ul. Kolejowa 3
tel: 228-86

Kedzierzyn-Koźl. 47-220
Pl. Wolności 1
tel: 350-01
    323-80
telex: 039297 mkz pl

Kolobrzeg 78-100
ul. Piastowska 4/2
tel: 63-40

Kielce 25-514
ul. Swietokrzyska 10a
tel: 437-51
telex: 0612204

Konin 62-500
ul. Bydgoska 6/13
tel: 240-56

Lublin 109
ul. Krolewska 3
tel: 229-79
    269-64
    230-36

Legnica 59-200
ul. Jordana 12
tel: 202-17
    295-06
telex: 0787320

Leszno 64-100
ul. Boleslawa Chrobrego 21
tel: 68-58

Lublin 59-30
Kombinat Górniczo-Hutniczy Miedzi
tel: 410-01
    w. 382
telex: 0787385

Lódź 90-058
ul. Sienkiewicza 63
tel: 340-62

Nysa 48-361
ul. Watowa 7
tel: 23-15
telex: 039400

Opole 45-066
ul. Reymonta 16
Przeds. Budown. Przew.
tel: 320-34
    w. 44,45
    322-01
    389-45
telex: 0733465

Olsztyn 10-542
ul. Dabrowszczaków 39
tel: 241-11
    w. 313
telex: 052215

Opoczno 26-300
ul. Kolberga 2
tel: 22-41
    30-50
telex: 884538

Plock 09-400
ul. Jachowicza 4
tel: 258-04
    287-88
    287-97
telex: 83640

Poznań 60-813
ul. Zwierzyniecka 15
tel: 468-19
telex: 0414225

Przemyśl 37-700
ul. Szczepanowskiego 2
tel: 56-56
telex: 0634313

Pila 64-920
ul. Buczka 14
tel: 41-44
telex: 047501

Rzeszów 35-002
Plac Zwyciestwa 4
tel: 386-81
    333-23
telex: 0633320

Radom 26-600
ul. Moniuszki
tel: 259-71
    279-95
telex: 067455

Szczecinek 78-400
ul. Zamkowa 11/12
tel: 434-44
telex: 0534357

Swinoujście 72-600
ul. Armii Czerwdnej 15
tel: 35-40

Suwalki 16-400
ul. Kościuszki 91
tel: 27-02
telex: 853138

Stalowa Wola 37-450
ul. Staszica 15b
tel: 203-01
    205-01
    w. 13-03
    235-95
telex: 062299

Szczecin 70-515
ul. Moniuszki
tel: 357-13
    440-01
telex: 0425695

Sieradz 98-200
Plac Swierczewskiego 6
tel: 30-88

Slupsk 76-200
ul. Lukasiewicza 1
tel: 74-48
telex: 0534307

Toruń 87-100
ul. Bydgoska 8
tel: 236-77
telex: 055297

Tychy /FSM/ 43-100
ul. Engelsa 3
tel: 27-28-21

Walbrzych 58-300
ul. 1-Maja 112
tel: 235-76
telex: 074557

Warsaw (Mazowsze region) 00-561
ul. Mokotowska 16-20
tel: 283-461/7
telex: 816077

Wloclawek 87-800
ul. Kilinskiejo 9
tel: 244-08

Wroclaw 50-412
ul. Mazowiecka 17
tel: 33320
telex: 0715500

Ziemia Sieradzka
Zduńska Wola 98-220
ul. Sieradzka 33
tel: 44-34

Ziélona Góra 65-036
ul. Niepodleglosci 32
tel: 57-56

Ziemia Podolska Siedlce 08-100
ul. Kochanowskiego 7
tel: 66-23